ST. GERARD
M

*"Thou art the God of my heart, and
the God that is my portion forever."*
—Psalm 72:26

SAINT GÉRARD MAJELLA.

St. Gerard Majella
1726-1755
Lay Brother of the Congregation
of the Most Holy Redeemer

ST. GERARD MAJELLA

THE WONDER-WORKER
AND
PATRON OF EXPECTANT MOTHERS

By

Fr. Edward Saint-Omer, C.SS.R.

"And the works that I do, he also shall do; and greater than these shall he do."
—John 14:12

TAN BOOKS AND PUBLISHERS, INC.
Rockford, Illinois 61105

Imprimi Potest: William G. Licking, C.SS.R.
                 Provincial
                 Baltimore
                 Feast of St. Gerard [Oct. 16], 1907

Nihil Obstat: Patrick J. Supple
                 Censor Librorum

Imprimatur: ✠ William Henry [O'Connell]
                 Archbishop of Boston
                 Boston

Published c. 1907 by Mission Church Press, Boston, Massachusetts under the title: *The Wonder-Worker of Our Days— The Life, Virtues, and Miracles of St. Gerard Majella, Lay-Brother of the Congregation of the Most Holy Redeemer*. Reproduced complete and unabridged from the Second Edition, with slight modernization of words and improvements in translation.

Library of Congress Catalog Card No.: 98-61400

ISBN 0-89555-630-8

Printed and bound in the United States of America.

TAN BOOKS AND PUBLISHERS, INC.
P.O. Box 424
Rockford, Illinois 61105
1999

"To the honor of the Most Holy and Undivided Trinity, for the exaltation of the Catholic Faith and for the spread of the Christian Religion, by the authority of Our Lord Jesus Christ, of the Blessed Apostles Peter and Paul and by Our own . . . We define and declare the Blessed Confessors Gerard Majella and Alexander Sauli to be Saints, and We enroll them in the catalogue of Saints . . ."

—Pope St. Pius X
December 11, 1904
(See p. 252.)

St. Gerard, pray for us.

PUBLISHER'S PREFACE

The incredible life of St. Gerard Majella has been a great inspiration to the entire Catholic Church for over 200 years, and yet his story may cause some readers to become discouraged about their own salvation. But this should not be.

As with so many great and notable Saints in the history of the Catholic Church, St. Gerard Majella is believed never to have committed a mortal sin; in fact, his spiritual advisers could not detect that he had ever committed even a venial sin. Undoubtedly, this level of sanctity was the basis for the many miracles that he worked during life, and even after death.

And yet we read in Father Saint-Omer's life of the Saint that he often had periods of great spiritual darkness, and even came close to despairing of his salvation. This fact could easily lead the reader to discouragement, for if St. Gerard, who was so very good, had periods of darkness, even to the point of despair, what about the vast majority of us, who are nowhere near so good, who oftentimes fall into sin, who perhaps even commit mortal sin, or who have in the past lived in mortal sin? Should not *we* be the ones inclined to despair? "If one who was so obviously holy and blessed by Almighty God was worried about his salvation, what chance do we have?" might well be our question.

vii

viii *St. Gerard Majella*

An attitude of concern, of course, is typical of all who are truly on the road to salvation. St. Peter, no less, gives us the clue to this seeming paradox of "sanctity combined with concern" when he says, "If the just man shall scarcely be saved, where shall the ungodly and the sinner appear?" (*1 Peter* 4:18). In other words, if those true Christians who are avoiding mortal sin and who are striving for Heaven shall barely be saved, what about *a*) the open sinners, who knowingly and blithely (it would seem) commit mortal sin, and *b*) the ungodly, who have no real concern for their salvation and who mainly pursue worldly goals? "Where shall they appear?" The point is that people living without the light of the Gospel of Jesus Christ are in darkness about their eternal salvation. Even regarding Catholics, the Curé of Ars could say, "Some people are so profoundly ignorant that they do not recognize a quarter of their ordinary sins."

This failure to recognize our sins arises from the spiritual darkness caused, on the one hand, by Original Sin, and on the other, by our own personal sins. When a person begins really to live by the teachings of Our Lord and to strive for perfection, there occur as a consequence moments wherein his mind penetrates the veil of this darkness, and in that spiritual insight, he perceives—if only for a brief time—the precarious state of man's salvation, that "we have all sinned and do need the glory of God." (*Rom.* 3:23). Such periodic moments of clear insight can cause us almost to despair, as St. Gerard nearly did on a number of occasions.

Far from causing us to despair, however, these moments of spiritual lucidity—wherein we perceive our great danger—should cause us joy. For as Holy Scripture repeats in several places, "The fear of the Lord is the beginning of wisdom." (*Psalm* 110:10; cf. also *Prov.* 15:33; *Eccles.* 1:20, 22, 25, 34; 19:18). St. Paul tells us, "With fear and trembling work out your salvation." (*Phil.* 2:12). When once we who are earnestly striving for salvation become concerned and "fearful," this means that the scales of blindness covering our spiritual insight are falling away and we are starting to see our situation as it really is vis-a-vis pleasing God and attaining our salvation! And the prospect is frightening, because we find ourselves, especially in our inclinations and motives, to be far from really good. All the greatest Saints had this perception, and they were humble as a result, for they could see their own weaknesses and shortcomings. That is the reason, when one starts to receive this insight, that confidence in God becomes such a necessary virtue.

The life of St. Gerard Majella throws these realities about the spiritual life into sharp focus. On the one hand, he was so good and worked so many miracles, and on the other, he was so profoundly concerned about his own salvation. Reading about this concern of his, one could say to himself, "What's the use? If St. Gerard had such trouble, I will never make it!" But that is exactly the wrong reaction. Why?

First of all, we must distinguish between ordinary and extraordinary Saints. You and I, probably, and most of us, are called to be *ordinary* Saints, people who work out our salvation pretty much in obscurity and, when we pass from this life, are forgotten by all save a few close loved ones. *Extraordinary* Saints are generally called by God to do some extraordinary work or to have their holiness manifested to the world as a great inspiration to others. St. Gerard, obviously, was an extraordinary Saint. The number of extraordinary Saints is relatively small, compared to the number who live in obscurity. But this does not mean that you and I cannot achieve great sanctity and find a high place in Heaven.

Sanctity depends on our interior state, upon the degree of our love of God, upon uniformity with His holy Will and upon the purity of our motives. Indeed, if we are so blessed as to gain Heaven, we shall likely find there in the highest places many who were obscure mothers and fathers and other lay people in this life.

St. Therese the Little Flower stands in both camps—ordinary and extraordinary. In life, her sanctity was unknown to the world, unknown even to many of the nuns in her Carmelite convent. But it was *not* unknown to her own sisters, who, after her death, helped make her known to the world. She was so tremendous that Pope St. Pius X could exclaim that she is the greatest Saint of modern times—she, a totally unknown nun who died at 24 and of whom a fellow sister commented to the effect: "What shall we ever find to say about Sr. Therese of the Child

Jesus in our announcement of her death to the other Carmelite convents?" Now the whole world knows her. (Just ask her for a favor!)

Notable in St. Gerard's life is the high level of sanctity he achieved in a relatively short time. He died at age 29. From this we can all take heart. For if we have till now delayed working seriously on our salvation, we can nonetheless make up for lost time—*and in a hurry*—if we are truly contrite, ardent, sincere and constant in our efforts at reparation, virtue and love of God. Plus, we have in St. Gerard Majella a great patron Saint. Not only is he "Patron of Expectant Mothers," for which he is famous the world over, but he is obviously one of those *universal* patron Saints, like St. Joseph, whom one can call upon in every need. Witness the great devotion to him that developed in Belgium. (Cf. page 237). Indeed, we could all make him our own personal "Patron Saint of Rapid Growth in Holiness"— of "holiness in a hurry," if you will.

Yes, God is honored by the greatness of His Saints, and He wants us to approach Him with all our needs through these heavenly friends of His, who in their lives loved Him so truly and so well that they have been "raised to the altars." The quintessential model of all Saints, of course, is Our Lady, whom Our Dear Lord wishes to honor and recognize at every turn and in all things, such that He allows all graces (theology teaches us) to come to us only through her. Yes, God wants to share His greatness, His goodness, His beneficence and His glory with His friends, the Saints and Holy Angels. As would a great, magnanimous earthly king, He wants to share His glory with His friends and servants who surround Him. Therefore, we can call upon St. Gerard Majella with utmost confidence. Surely all expectant mothers should do so, of whom he is the special patron, but also all other faithful people, in whatever need they might have.

St. Alphonsus Liguori—St. Gerard's spiritual father as founder of the Congregation of the Most Holy Redeemer—outlived St. Gerard by 32 years; yet in miracles and lustrous sanctity, St. Gerard would seem to have o'ertopped even that eminent Doctor of the Church and his own superior, a man whom the whole Church knows and who is the most widely published author in history!

Yes, Dear Reader, the least can indeed become the greatest in the wonderful, paradoxical reality of the Catholic Faith! And from the life of St. Gerard Majella, not only can we derive great inspiration at the goodness and mercy of God as shown through the life and ministry of so great and extraordinary a Saint, but we can also be assured in all confidence that we too can ourselves rise to high sanctity by employing the same humble means used by St. Gerard Majella and all other Saints, viz., prayer, penance, sacrifice, good works—and *confidence* in Almighty God, who desires our salvation above all else.

Thomas A. Nelson
Publisher
December 17, 1998

A NOTE TO THE READER
From the Edition published c. 1907

This biography was taken by Father Saint-Omer from the beautiful Italian edition which appeared at the Beatification of the great Servant of God entitled *Vita del Beato Gerardo Majella . . . Roma, Tipografia Vaticana,* 1893. We have here reproduced it in full [translating it from Fr. Saint-Omer's French], with the addition only of the chapter on the glorification of the Saint.

"We do not pretend," wrote Father Saint-Omer in 1893, "to put forth a learned work. Our intention is to offer to the public an inexpensive book, so desirous are we to see the life of Brother Gerard introduced into the humble homes of the poor for their encouragement and edification. Our hero was a child of the people, an apprentice, a servant, a workman, a humble lay brother, whom grace transformed into a Saint. If we put aside the purely gratuitous supernatural gifts which God gives to whom He pleases, what Gerard became, every child of the people may become as well as he, by the practice of virtue, by suffering and by conformity to the will of God."

Preface to The Second Edition

SOME REMARKS ON THE MARVELOUS IN THE LIFE OF ST. GERARD

Sound reason, reason unbiased by prejudice, cannot but admit the *possibility* of miracles in general; and when a miraculous *fact* is proved, to reject it because it *is* miraculous and inexplicable to our feeble intelligence is not the part of a wise man, since the purely natural order is full of facts admitted by everyone, although no one, not even men of genius, can explain them; for instance, the germination of seed. Now, a miraculous fact is proved just as an ordinary one.

We have said that right reason cannot help admitting the possibility of a miracle: "No man making use of his reason," writes Cardinal Dechamps, "will reject the marvelous found in the Lives of the Saints under the plea of impossibility. Only the unthinking dare to say that miracles are impossible and—by reasoning as absurd as it is impious—to put a limit to the almighty power of God. Miracles are phenomena which interrupt the laws of nature and surpass the force of all natural causes. Reason alone is needed to make a man understand that God, whose power is infinite, can, when it so pleases Him, interrupt nature's course directly by Himself or indirectly by the ministry of His creatures." (*Dissertation upon the Marvelous in the Lives of the Saints.*)

St. Augustine, that sublime genius, had said long before: "All nature is full of miracles. We are not astonished at them because we are used to seeing them; their repetition makes them familiar to our eyes. Behold why God has reserved to Himself others out of the course of nature, that they may strike us by their novelty." (*De Civit. Dei,* L.X).

But for the Christian, the possibility of a miracle is not a question; it is a point of Faith which he professes every day when he says: "I believe in God, the Father Almighty," and which springs from these words of the Gospel: "No word shall be impossible with God" (*Luke* 1:37); and from these others: "He that believeth in me, the works that I do, he also shall do, and greater than these shall he do." (*John* 14:12).

But is it indeed certain that God has at times performed miracles? Here as above, the affirmative is of Faith for every Christian. What, in truth, is the whole history of the people of God—a history written under the dictation of the Holy Ghost—but a series of miracles—the plagues of Egypt, the passage through the Red Sea, the pillar of cloud, the manna which fell from Heaven every morning for forty years in sufficient quantity to feed several million, etc.?

Can God communicate to Saints the power to work miracles? Yes, since He is all-powerful. In fact, when a miracle is performed, it is always God who performs it at the request of a Saint.

Has He at times done so? Yes, answers Holy Scripture. How many miracles were performed by the Apostles and their disciples under the eyes of all! To enumerate some: a paralytic cured at the gate of the Temple, Tabitha raised from the dead, the shadow alone of St. Peter curing the sick, etc. Long ago it was said: "To suppose that the pagan world would have become Christian without being influenced thereto by the sight of great and numerous miracles is to suppose a miracle greater than those that fill the lives of the Saints."

Did God give St. Gerard this power of performing miracles? Yes, the history of his life proclaims it, a history as credible as any other history—that of Napoleon, for instance. The facts related had witnesses who were able to prove for themselves their genuineness, for the *Life of Brother Gerard* [by Tannoia, a contemporary of St. Gerard] appeared a short time after his death. Besides, the Acts of Beatification may be taken as a guarantee of their evidence. It is an enormous folio volume containing the depositions of a crowd of sworn witnesses.

In fine, the Holy See itself has already juridically confirmed some of those miraculous facts. It first submitted them to the most severe examination, by minutely interrogating the witnesses and requiring the opinion of the most able physicians. It proceeded with its proverbial slowness in order to take time to examine the cause, and only after these proceedings did it pronounce.

Never do our tribunals of justice act with so much consideration nor take so many precautions, even in questions of life or death.

But some say that the marvelous in the life of St. Gerard is so extraordinary that it scandalizes even good Catholics! Scandalizes them? No. Surprises them? Yes. They are astonished, but not scandalized, because they know that God is all-powerful, that He is the Master of His gifts and that His love for souls most faithful to Him sometimes far exceeds the greatest maternal tenderness.

After all that has been said, I ask whether there is a man of sense who will exclaim: "The marvelous plays too great a part in the life of this Saint. I will have none of it!" No, rather he will kneel down humbly before his Creator and say: "O Thou to Whom everything is possible, Thou art worthy to be our God! I adore Thee! Have pity on me, dust and ashes that I am!"

CONTENTS

—Part Four—
THE SUPERNATURAL GIFTS OF ST. GERARD

—Part Five—
DEATH AND GLORIFICATION OF ST. GERARD

ST. GERARD MAJELLA

"*So that even there were brought from his body to the sick, handkerchiefs and aprons, and the diseases departed from them, and the wicked spirits went out of them.*"
—Acts 19:12

—Part One—

ST. GERARD MAJELLA'S
LIFE IN THE WORLD

1. THE SAINTLY CHILD

THE Life that we are now writing is a long chain of marvels. When turning its pages, the reader will recall the act of faith which he makes every day: "I believe in God, the Father Almighty," also the words of the Gospel, "No word shall be impossible with God" (*Luke* 1:37), and this promise of Jesus Christ, "He that believeth in me, the works that I do, he also shall do, and greater than these shall he do" (*John* 14:12), for the Holy Spirit declares, "God is wonderful in His saints." (*Ps.* 67:36).

The blessed child whose virtues we are going to portray was born in April, 1726 at Muro, a little village about sixty miles south of Naples. His father, a tailor by trade, was Dominico Majella, and his mother was Benedetta Galella—both admirable for their thoroughly Christian life. The newborn babe received in Baptism the name of Gerard. From the very cradle, he gave evidence of the high sanctity to which God destined him, for never did he weep, never did he demand nourishment by his cries, as do other children. On certain days, he even refused the maternal breast, a presage of the severe abstinence which he kept his whole life long. Benedetta wondered. She would say to him tenderly: "God bless you, dear child!" Prepared by grace from his earliest years, he found his only amusement in the little practices of devotion suited to his age. His two sisters, Brigida and Anna Elizabetta, tell us that Gerard's only attraction when a child was to make little altars and imitate the ceremonies of divine worship. He used to place on a table the pictures of the Saints, that of St. Michael in particular, and pass and repass before them, inclining and bowing. Then, kneeling down, he would recite some prayers, striking his breast or singing the pious canticles that he had heard in church. His growing piety astonished and delighted all who saw it.

Gerard's life convinces us of this truth, that God finds His delights among the children of men and in converse with them. A short distance from Muro stands the chapel of Capotignano, where a statue of the Blessed Virgin Mary holding the Infant Jesus in her arms is venerated. When Gerard was not yet six years old, led no doubt by a heavenly hand, he made his way to this sanctuary. Scarcely had he knelt down when the little Jesus, leaving His Mother's arms, came to play with him and gave him a little loaf of extreme whiteness. The child joyfully carried the present home to his mother. In great surprise, she asked: "Who gave it to you?"

"It was a beautiful lady's Child with whom I have

been playing." Attracted by the divine charms of his heavenly Friend, Gerard ran every morning to the chapel, and each time the Infant God came down to play with him and to present to him a little white loaf. Brigida's curiosity urged her one day to follow her little brother, and unknown to him, she became a witness of the prodigy. The prudent mother, Benedetta, did likewise and saw the same thing.

Following the example of her Son, the Blessed Virgin also desired to give Gerard the miraculous bread. The child himself revealed to us this secret. Going one day into the chapel with his mother, pointing to the statue of the Blessed Virgin, he said: "Mama, there is the Lady who gave me bread more than once, and there is the Child with whom I have played." Years after, when he had become a Redemptorist, his sister Brigida having come to see him, he said to her with his usual simplicity: "I now know that it was the Infant Jesus who gave me the little white loaves."

"Well," replied his sister smiling, "come again to see the Child."

"At present," said Gerard, "I find Him wherever I wish."

This was not the only miraculous fact in the childhood of St. Gerard. One day he was playing at forming a procession with some children of his own age. He attached to a tree a little cross that he had made and called upon his young friends to venerate it. But lo, a prodigy! The tree became sparkling with light, to the great amazement of the good people of Muro, and the little Child Jesus, coming down from it, again bestowed upon Gerard the tiny white loaf that He was accustomed to give him.

Toward the age of eight, this child so favored by Jesus was already hungering for the Eucharistic Bread. One day when at Mass, he went up to the Holy Table to receive Communion with the other Faithful. The celebrant, seeing him so young, passed him by, and the child retired in tears. But on the night following, St. Michael the Archangel comforted him by bringing him the Bread of Angels. It was for this reason that Gerard preserved during his whole life a tender devotion toward this holy Archangel.

This was not the only time that Benedetta's favored son was communicated miraculously. A priest, finding him one day kneeling near the altar, asked him what he was doing there. "A little Child," answered Gerard, "came out of the Tabernacle and gave me Holy Communion."

This favor, so rare in the lives of even the most privileged Saints, Gerard merited, doubtless by his heroic temperance. Who would believe it? This little child took scarcely enough nourishment to support life. His mother, sometimes alarmed at the fact, used to say to her friends: "My son eats almost nothing. For whole days he does not touch food."

2. THE SAINTLY SCHOLAR

WHILE still very young, Gerard was sent to school in his native place, Muro. In a short time he learned to read and write, to count and even to express himself with facility. His special love was for the Catechism and all that concerned religion. Far from indulging in the levity of other children during class hours, he was quiet, silent and attentive to his lessons. His docility and application were so great that his teacher regarded him with tender affection and called him his "delight." As soon as school was over, little Gerard promptly returned home, carefully shunning the company of such of his fellow scholars as were giddy and unreserved in their speech.

It was above all in the Holy Place that the pious child of Muro appeared most admirable. His recollected exterior made him look like an Angel. All the sacred services of the Church attracted him wonderfully. His devotion during the Holy Sacrifice of the Mass was extraordinary in a child of his age, and he seemed to be entirely absorbed in the great Mystery celebrated at the altar. At the moment of Consecration, he bowed profoundly to the ground. His angelic piety, so charming to all who witnessed it, won the Heart of God and was recompensed by the apparition of the Infant Jesus. Frequently during the Holy Sacrifice, Gerard beheld on the altar the Infant God under a visible form. His heart was inundated with joy, but when he saw Him disappear at the priest's Communion, he shed tears of sorrow.

Even at this early age, he experienced a supernatural attraction for the House of God. It was his Paradise of delights. Just as the child is happy at the mother's side, so this holy boy found his greatest satisfaction at the foot of the Tabernacle. When the evening bell called the people to visit the Blessed Sacrament, he hastened to the church, taking with him his young companions: "Let us go," he would say to them, "let us go to visit Jesus Christ, who has made Himself a prisoner for us!"

This tender love for Our Lord was joined to a filial devotion to the Queen of Heaven. He recited her Rosary daily and performed different penances in her honor, especially at the approach of her feasts. For her part, Mary treated him as her privileged child. One day among others, Gerard took part in a pilgrimage from Muro to Caposele. But scarcely was the little pilgrim on his knees before the miraculous picture of the Mother of God than he was ravished in ecstasy, as if Mary had appeared to him.

Despite his youth, he was already favored with the gift of miracles. The care of a lamb had been confided to him. It happened that some robbers stole it and killed it. The child—seeing that its loss was a great annoyance to his parents, since the animal did not belong to them—said: "Be assured the lamb will come back." Then he began to pray, and soon, by a prodigy of the Divine Goodness, the little creature was restored to its lawful owner.

Toward his tenth year, the holy child made his First Communion. His seraphic fervor filled with deep emotion all who saw him. From that time, the Eucharist became the food of his soul and the charm of his heart. His confessor hesitated not to grant him the favor of communicating every other day.

This angel of earth soon understood that he could not share in the glory of Jesus without first participating in His dolorous Passion. Smitten with the holy folly of the Cross, he imposed upon himself a cruel scourging as the price of every one of the Communions that he received. God Himself was leading him on the way of Calvary.

3. THE SAINTLY APPRENTICE

ABOUT this time Gerard lost his father. This obliged his mother to place him as an apprentice to a tailor named Pannuto. The young apprentice devoted himself entirely to his work, meanwhile giving still more care to a faithful correspondence to grace and to following his attraction for prayer. Under the action of the Holy Spirit on his soul, he was sometimes seen ravished out of himself, and again, more freely to pour out his heart before God, he would hide under the worktable.

His master loved him and was careful not to reprove him. Not so, however, the foreman. He looked upon such piety with a suspicious eye. One day, he dragged Gerard from the place in which he was praying and began to beat him severely. "Strike,

strike!" said the holy apprentice, "you are right in doing so."

On another occasion, the cruel man dealt him blows so violent that Gerard fell unconscious to the ground. Pannuto, appearing unexpectedly on the scene, indignantly demanded an explanation. The foreman, pointing to his victim, replied, "Let him say. He knows very well."

"I fell from the table," said the youth gently. Another time, the brutal man gave him a rude blow on the ear, to which Gerard only responded by a quiet smile. "What! You are laughing!" exclaimed the barbarian in wrath, and seizing an iron instrument, he pitilessly struck the boy. The tender martyr, throwing himself at his feet, said in a tone full of sweetness: "I freely forgive you for the love of Jesus Christ."

One morning, Gerard happened to arrive a little late, which fact furnished a pretext to this madman to beat him with fury. A sweet smile was all that he drew from the child. "What! You are laughing!" cried his infuriated assailant. "Tell me, why are you laughing?"

"It is because the hand of God has struck me," answered the angel of patience.

Gerard never complained to his master of the bad treatment he received in his house. Pannuto regarded him with admiration. One day, he secretly followed the youth to church and there saw him after a long prayer lick with his tongue the pavement from where he was kneeling to the foot of the altar and then fall into ecstasy. From that moment he venerated him as a Saint and dismissed the foreman who had so persecuted him.

The following incident is a new proof of the patience of the young tailor. One day as he was passing through a lonely place, the sound of his footsteps frightened away a bird just as a sportsman was going to fire. The latter fell upon him furiously and dealt him a blow on the face. Faithful to the word of the Divine Master, Gerard presented to him the other cheek. The man in his anger beheld in that act only an insult to himself and redoubled his bad treatment. Fortunately, Pannuto's son happened to come along and interceded for the innocent youth. The sportsman was appeased, and passing suddenly from anger to admiration, he went about making known everywhere the virtue of the young apprentice.

About the time when the grapes were ripening, Pannuto asked Gerard to go one night with his son to guard the vine against robbers. The servant of God, desirous of meditating on the Passion, made a little cross, placed around it some tiny candles and began to chant the *Miserere*. Suddenly, the thatched shed that sheltered them caught fire. "What have you done?" exclaimed Pannuto's son. "It is nothing," responded Gerard quietly, and as he made the Sign of the Cross, the fire was instantly extinguished.

Tradition relates another miracle wrought by the Saint when he was with Pannuto. The latter finished a coat for someone. But it proved a misfit; it was too short. Seeing the embarrassment of both the tradesman and the customer, Gerard said: "Let me do it. It is nothing." And taking the coat in one hand, he drew it down with the other and at once gave it back widened and lengthened, a perfect fit in every way.

The young lover of the Crucified felt that he was not made for the world. He was drawn by a divine and imperative attraction toward the religious life. He went, therefore, to present himself at the convent of the Capuchins of San Menna, where he had an uncle, a very learned man, named Father Bonaventura de Muro. But Gerard was rejected on account of his poor health. On bidding him good-bye, his uncle, touched at seeing him so poorly clad, gave him a new coat. But hardly had Gerard left the convent when he met a poor man in rags and bestowed upon him the coat just received. His uncle reproached him, but the saintly young man replied: "I have given it to one more needy than I."

4. THE SAINTLY DOMESTIC

WHILE awaiting God's hour for his entrance into religion, Gerard, then about sixteen, took service in the episcopal residence of Msgr. Albini, the Bishop of Lacedonia. He was a man of great merit, but of a hasty temper. God made use of him to exercise His youthful servant in the practice of the most sublime Christian virtues. Complaints, scoldings, humiliations, excessive labor—the humble son of Benedetta was of a nature to support it all. The respectful silence that he kept during and after the most unjust corrections, his manner of receiving them—eyes cast down and countenance serene—his cheerfulness always sweet and amiable; his obedience to the least sign, and his love of labor—everything in him already denoted the heroic virtue of a Saint.

Despite his labors, Gerard continued in his new home the astonishing mortifications to which he was accustomed. One day the physician, noticing the pallor of his countenance, asked him whether he was sick. "I am well," answered Gerard, smiling. The physician, incredulous, touched him on the breast and found that he was wearing a rough hairshirt.

Affable toward all, good to the poor, tender toward the sick, the holy youth knew only one enemy, and that was himself. For his own nourishment, he allowed himself only a little bread and rarely any vegetables. Whatever else was given him in the kitchen, he reserved for the poor and sick.

All who met him passing through the streets of the city were struck by his modest appearance. "Little Gerard," they used to say, "is not a man; he is an Angel, he is a Saint." But what edified the beholder above all else was his recollection, his piety when in the presence of the Blessed Sacrament. When his occupations permitted, he was sure to be found in the Cathedral, paying court to the King of kings. At the sight of so edifying an example, many resolved to pay a daily visit to the Saviour in His Sacrament of Love.

God, who loves simple and pure souls, was pleased to fulfill the least desires of this earthly angel. One day, Gerard was so unfortunate as to let the key of the Bishop's room fall down the well. Foreseeing the chagrin that this accident would cause the prelate, the poor boy was himself greatly troubled. What should he do to recover the key? In his perplexity, he began to pray. Suddenly, filled with confidence, he ran to get a statue of the Infant Jesus, which he let down into the well, saying, "It is for Thee, Lord, to bring me the key, that the Bishop may not be put to trouble." O prodigy! In the sight of a crowd of bystanders, Gerard drew up the Infant Jesus holding in His hand the lost key. This well was thenceforth called, "Little Gerard's Well."

Three years after Gerard's entrance into the service of the Bishop, the latter died. This was in 1744. The boy wept over the death of his master. "Alas! I have lost my best friend," he exclaimed, so eager was he for mortifications.

5. THE SAINTLY WORKMAN

AFTER the death of his master, Gerard returned to Muro, thinking to earn his living by his trade. But as he had not worked at it for three years, he entered upon an apprenticeship once more, with a very good man named Vitus Mennona, whose home he perfumed with the fragrance of his virtues.

Vitus held him in an esteem that never diminished. He loved to recount the following prodigy: One day, a woman belonging to his family went to wash the linen at a fountain about a mile from the city. Gerard accompanied her. Suddenly, a deluge of rain forced them to seek shelter in a neighboring hut. As it grew late and the rain still continued, the poor woman began to lament and say, "How shall we get home?" At these words, Gerard stepped outside the door and, full of confidence in God, raised his eyes to Heaven, exclaiming, "Lord, what shall we do?" The words were scarcely out of his mouth before the rain ceased, the weather cleared up and they returned home.

His second apprenticeship over, Gerard took up his abode in his mother's home. Work was never wanting to him, his perfect honesty attracting many customers. With his mother's consent, he divided his earnings into three parts: one for the family, one for the poor and the third for the souls in Purgatory. Benedetta sometimes complained of the liberality of her son, but he would say, "Fear nothing, Mother, God will provide for all our needs."

He loved, above all, to work for the poor. One day, God manifested to him how pleased He was with his charity. A poor man had sent him some material for a garment, but far less than it would take to make it. In the hands of the servant of God, it so increased that when the garment was finished, some of the material remained over. The miraculous surplus was conscientiously returned to the man.

He frequently had Masses celebrated for the Suffering Souls. "They, too, are poor," he used to say. "They earnestly call for our help." When work was not as brisk as usual, he was broken-hearted. He then ate only dry bread, that he might be able to assist the poor of the good God and his dear souls in Purgatory.

But what he gave, he took from himself, for he always had at heart the practice of mortification, and especially that of the taste. He ate so little that his existence seemed a miracle. When pressed to eat, he would reply: "I am not hungry." He was ingenious, also, in discovering means to stifle the cravings of hunger. His mother asked him one day what he did with the roots that he always carried in his pocket. "They serve," he answered, "to chase away appetite." Benedetta shed bitter tears over the austerities of her son, but her friends consoled her by telling her that he was a child of Heaven.

At the age of twenty, Gerard went for about a month to San Fele, a little town not far from Muro. He had been invited to do so by one of his townsmen, who had opened there a school for the higher branches. This man had need of a tailor to attend to the clothes of his boarding pupils. His name was Malpiedi.

It would be difficult to imagine all that the Saint had to endure in his house. The pupils, with precocious malice, were ingenious in tormenting him, not only by insults, but by blows brutally multiplied. In the midst of the most inhuman treatment, which was often very prolonged, the holy young man uttered only the words, "Stop now!" or "O God!" or "What have I done to you?" And who would believe that

Malpiedi himself, wishing doubtless to see how far the patience of the humble workman would go, subjected him several times to the punishment of the whip. But the pain never drew a complaint from this soul thirsting for martyrdom.

6. THE SERAPH OF MURO

LOVE assimilates lovers. Deeply moved at beholding Jesus Christ treated during His Passion as a fool, Gerard under the influence of a supernatural inspiration, determined to imitate folly. This holy folly of divine love cost him dearly.

The children ran after him in the streets of Muro, made sport of him, said a thousand insulting things to him, threw mud in his face and loaded him with blows. Some of them went so far as even to bind him with cords, drag him along the stony road and hold him up as a spectacle of derision to the multitude. Gerard bore all their cruel treatment, not as a fool, but as a Saint. With smiling and radiant countenance, he said: "All this is little for the love of Jesus Christ, who became like unto a fool of love for my sake." It was at that moment the Lord placed upon his lips prophetic words: "You despise me now, but a time will come when you will hold me in honor and kiss my hand."

In the excess of his love for Jesus suffering, Gerard wished to undergo like Him the punishment of scourging. "Often," relates Felix Farenga, the Saint's friend and confidant, "very often, I had to tie him to a post and strike him over his bare shoulders with wet cords. He bore it with joy, and when I expressed my repugnance at striking him so long, he earnestly begged me to continue, until his body was one wound and his blood flowed on all sides."

The young lover of the Cross made use of another means to crucify himself. He had himself suspended from a beam, head downward, over some smoldering rags, that the smoke might torture his eyes and throat. "We ought to suffer," he used to say, "to please Him who suffered so much for us."

This torment of smoke seems to have had for him a special attraction. One day, at the Stella house, he bent down under the mantlepiece just as a volume of thick smoke was mounting up from the fire. "Gerard, what are you doing there?" asked someone. "Smoke is good for beautiful eyes," he answered gaily.

In all these circumstances, Gerard followed an interior attraction which was the manifest expression of God's designs over him. They who inflicted on him such torture knew him well, and it was their good faith that excused them for having made him suffer so cruelly.

It is customary in Italy to re-enact the scenes of the Passion. One of these pious spectacles was organized in the Cathedral of Muro, but someone was lacking to represent Jesus Crucified. Gerard obtained this favor. At the appointed hour, the Cathedral doors were opened, and Gerard was seen hanging on the cross, his arms extended and as if in agony. At this sight, the people burst into tears, and Benedetta, unprepared to behold her son in such a situation, uttered a cry of anguish and fell fainting.

If Gerard was smitten with the sublime folly of the Cross, he was not less so with that of the Eucharist. As during the day, he could not fully satisfy his heart, obliged as he was to labor for his living, he indemnified himself at night. The sacristan of the Cathedral, a relative of his, readily gave him the keys of the Holy Place. There Gerard, seraph of love, found his delight in spending whole nights in adoration at the foot of the holy Tabernacle.

The Heart of the good Master, ravished by the touching simplicity and holy folly of the pious young man, gave him to understand, in order to try him, that He looked upon his conduct as worthy of a fool. "But Thou, O my good Jesus," responded Gerard with holy familiarity, in which the most ardent love and the most filial respect were mingled, "hast not Thou given me the first example of folly by thus imprisoning Thyself for me?"

On another occasion, the Divine Master reproached him lovingly for the apparent extravagance of his piety. "O my God," replied Gerard, "how canst Thou address such a reproach to me? Is it not Thyself Who hast taught me these follies?" He would have desired to inflame the universe with the burning ardor that consumed his own heart for the Blessed Sacrament. How often were these words heard to escape his lips: "Come, let us go to see Jesus, our Prisoner of Love!"

Hell was enraged at such piety. One morning, as Gerard was about to enter the Cathedral, the demon rushed upon him in the form of a horrible mastiff, barking furiously and seemingly about to devour him. The Saint made the Sign of the Cross, and the monster vanished. One night, Satan threw upon him a statue, which after wounding his arm, began to run after him in the church, as if it were alive. Unshaken in his confidence in Jesus, Gerard went on with his prayer and thus chased away the enemy.

His devotion to the Queen of Heaven was incomparable. If he knelt to pray before her statue or picture, he could not tear himself away. He loved to repeat: "The Madonna has stolen my heart, and I have made her a present of it." The mere thought of her or the sound of her name made his heart thrill with love.

A novena was celebrated at Muro in honor of the Immaculate Conception. Gerard, whose joy it was to assist at all the sacred services, had been on his knees for a long time. Suddenly, yielding to an irresistible inspiration of grace, he arose in the presence of the crowd, his countenance inflamed, and going up to the statue of Mary, placed a ring on its finger, exclaiming in a loud voice: "Behold me betrothed to the Madonna!" By this he desired to signify the consecration of his virginity to the Virgin of virgins, or to speak more properly, the betrothal of his virginity with that of Mary. He was so faithful to his engagement that he ever preserved unsullied the lily of chastity and the robe of baptismal innocence. His directors were unanimous in calling him an angel of purity.

It was about this time that Gerard consoled a poor mother by curing with the Sign of the Cross her child who had fallen into boiling water and whose heartrending cries touched all hearts with pity.

Another time, when passing before a building, he saw that the laborers were disconcerted because the beams were not long enough to reach from one wall to the other. The servant of God told the men to pull them with ropes. The workmen obeyed, and the beams immediately lengthened to the dimensions desired.

Gerard was not for the world, and the world was irksome to him. Not being able to obtain admission among the Capuchins, he formed the project of retiring into the solitude of some mountain, far from the sight of men. There he would divide his time between prayer, labor and penance, living on herbs and roots, as did the ancient Fathers of the Desert. A young man, fervent like himself, offered to accompany him. Their plan of life was hardly put into execution when obedience constrained them to abandon it.

Gerard was now twenty-two years old. God, who did not will him to be an anchorite, but a lay brother of the Congregation of the Most Holy Redeemer, was not slow in opening the way for him. In August, 1748, Father Garzilli passed through Muro with Brother Onofrio. Scarcely did Gerard see them when he felt inspired to join them. They told him that their Institute was not suitable for him on account of the rigor of its Rule and that his frail health would not permit him to observe it. "But that is precisely what I am seeking," replied the austere young man.

The next year, the Redemptorists gave the exercises of the mission at Muro with marvelous success. Gerard, enraptured by the zeal and holiness of the missionaries, became so attached to them that he could not quit their house. He spoke of his vocation to Father Cafaro, the Superior, and begged for admittance to the Institute. The Father, seeing him so slight, judged him unsuited to the life of a lay brother and advised him to renounce his design. This refusal did not discourage Gerard. He renewed his petition, but in vain. Benedetta, on her side, did all in her power to persuade her son not to leave her. "My son," she would say to him weeping and making allusion to the scene in the Cathedral related above, "my son, I entreat you by the pain that you caused me when I saw you on the cross; give me not this new sorrow." His sisters united with his mother to dissuade him from his design. They went so far as to lock him up. But faithful to his vocation, the prisoner, by the aid of the sheets from his bed, escaped by the window. He left a note to this effect: "I am going to become a Saint. Think no more of me."

On leaving his mother's house, Gerard ran after the Fathers, who had gone to give a mission at Rionero, and in the most humble and touching manner reiterated his petition. "Try me first," he repeated in a suppliant tone and shedding a torrent of tears, "try me first, and then you can send me away. If you do not receive me," he added, "you will see me every day begging alms at the convent gate." His admirable firmness softened Father Cafaro, who decided to give him a trial. He sent him to the convent of Iliceto, bearing with him a letter to the Father who was holding his place. It began with these words: "I am sending you a useless brother."

—Part Two—

ST. GERARD MAJELLA'S
LIFE IN RELIGION

1. THE SAINTLY NOVICE

O^N the 17th of May, 1749, a young man worn
out by fatigue knocked at the convent gate at
Iliceto. He was tall and slender, his face oval, the
forehead high and broad, his cheeks hollow, com-
plexion pale, bones projecting, his eyes modestly cast
down, his demeanor simple and his manner attrac-
tive. Heavenly joy and an unspeakable, angelic light
shone on his features. He had the appearance of a
man habituated to suffering and to the contemplation of a world superior to ours. Energy appeared
to be his dominant characteristic. This young man
was Gerard.

As soon as ever he had been admitted into the
Congregation, he had set out for Iliceto, and so
desirous was he to reach the house of God that he
made the whole journey in a day. When he learned
that the convent was dedicated to the miraculous
Virgin, honored under the title "Our Lady of
Consolation," his happiness was increased. He hastened to cast himself at the foot of her altar to thank

her for his vocation and to protest that he wished to live and die under her maternal care.

The convent, built in a solitude a couple of miles from the city of Iliceto, had been founded by Blessed Felix of Corsano of the Order of St. Augustine. It had been for a long time unoccupied when St. Alphonsus, yielding to the insistence of the Bishop of Bovino, but still more to the attraction exerted over his heart by the statue of Mary, established there his religious. It was in this holy hermitage that Gerard, the humble servant of Christ, was to pass the greater part of his religious life.

When Father Cafaro returned from the mission at Rionero, he found that his candidate was far from being the useless brother that he had at first thought. The Fathers and Brothers, one and all, praised his diligence in work, his piety and his virtue. He was, therefore, admitted to the rank of postulant. The good young man never ceased to bless the Mother of God and to kiss the walls of her sanctuary, so lively were the joy and gratitude of his heart.

He began at once a scrupulous observance of the paternal and sanctifying rules* established by St.

_____

*The following was, in few words, the daily schedule of the lay brothers: 4:30 Rising, 5:00 Meditation, 5:30 Holy Mass, 11:45 Particular Examen, 12:00 Dinner and Recreation, 1:30 Visit to the Blessed Sacrament and the third part of the Rosary, 3:00 Spiritual Reading, 3:30 Meditation, 6:30 Benediction and Way of the Cross, 7:00 Meditation, 7:30 Supper and Recreation, 9:00 Night Prayers.

During the day, everyone had to fulfill the employment assigned him. The lay brothers could go out, either to accom-

Alphonsus for the lay brothers. He chose for his
director Father Cafaro, a religious of eminent holiness. This man of God was not slow to perceive that
the Holy Spirit was conducting His disciple by
extraordinary ways and that He enlightened him on
the highest mysteries.

Some months after his entrance, Gerard received
the religious habit and began a first novitiate of six
months, according to the custom of the Institute with
regard to lay brothers. Never was there seen a novice
more fervent or one that better comprehended the
excellence of his vocation. The following note written by Gerard is a proof of it:

God has placed me in a paradise of delights.

Know, O Gerard, that the Lord has withdrawn thee from the world, and has placed
thee, a new Adam, in this paradise of the
Congregation, in order that thou mayest put
into practice the precepts and counsels of His
Gospel contained in the holy Rules. Woe to
thee if thou dost transgress them! Thy chas-

pany the Fathers in their visits to the sick, or even at times for
recreation. They were allowed three Communions per week, one
day of retreat every month and three days in each of the Ember
weeks. A spiritual prefect was assigned them in every house.
The Brothers were in everything treated like the Fathers, all
being looked upon as children of the same family. They shared
the same table, enjoyed the same privileges of the perfectly
common life. All may easily arrive at the interior life and holiness by uniting the spirit of prayer with love of labor.

tisement will be expulsion from the Institute
(from this may God preserve thee!) and consequently, thou wilt be damned.

Gerard had resolved to become a Saint. But the
holiness of a lay brother does not consist only in
prayer, meditation and other exercises of piety. It
consists also and principally in labor. It is to this
that God calls him. He should, by praying and directing all his actions to the glory of God, concur by
generous labor in the work of the Heavenly Father,
that the end of the Institute may be attained.

Our Saint perfectly understood this truth. If his
life in the world had been admirable, that which he
led in Religion was still more so. While doing the
work of four, as his confreres attest, he knew how
to unite perfectly the contemplative with the active
life. For some time he was employed in the culti-
vation of the garden. This occupation, so unaccus-
tomed to him who was a tailor by trade, he certainly
found most fatiguing. But regardless of that, he used
to take upon himself the tasks imposed on others.
"Let me do it," he would say gaily, "let me do it. I
am the youngest. You go and rest." The more menial
the occupation, the dearer it was to his humility.
Every kind of work was pleasing to him, above all
that which was considered low. In one word, he
seemed to have espoused fatigue, and he grieved at
not having it.

The fervent novice, already a model of regular
observance, was chiefly in love with obedience,

which he regarded as the essence of the religious life. He longed to practice it in all its fullness, in all its perfection, looking upon God in his superiors and the will of God in their orders. His favorite maxim was, "Do always and in everything the will of God." Hence these words that he loved to repeat: "Will of God! Will of God! Oh how happy is he who knows how to will the will of God!" This maxim, of which he never lost sight, made of him a Saint of obedience.

Toward the end of his novitiate, his virtue was subjected to a rude trial. All the Fathers having gone to the mission at Melfi, the government of the convent was confided to a young professed afflicted with one of those dreadful mental disorders which render a person altogether unfit for the religious life. No circumstance had as yet occurred to give evidence of his mental state. As soon as St. Alphonsus discovered it, however, he hastened to dismiss him.

It seemed as if Providence had permitted the temporary admission of this person expressly to try and make manifest the virtue of the Saint. Unreasonable and capricious to a degree, he had taken an aversion to Gerard. All day long he pursued him with cruel reproaches, severe and unmerited corrections, imposing on him hard penances, frequent fasts on bread and water and even making him trace with his tongue on the pavement from forty to sixty Signs of the Cross. This painful trial lasted a whole month and ended in the good brother's having his tongue so torn that sometimes the pavement was stained with blood. The holy novice endured all with invincible patience; not a complaint escaped his lips; not a shadow of repugnance altered the serenity of his countenance. His confreres, moved to tears at the recital of such torments and filled with admiration for such virtue, said among themselves: "Either this brother is a fool, or he is a great Saint." Yes, Gerard was a Saint, smitten with the holy folly of the Cross.

From gardener, Gerard became sacristan. No employment could better suit a soul like his devoured with zeal for the House of the Lord. He took such care of the sacred ornaments, the church was kept so scrupulously clean, such beautiful order reigned everywhere that fifty years after his death they still recalled it with admiration.

Once he got permission to have a pyx made for the Blessed Sacrament. The goldsmith to whom he had given the order delayed so long the execution of the work that Gerard was quite worn out with him. After expostulating with him in vain, Gerard said to him: "You show no desire to make the pyx. Very well! I am sorry for you. God will punish you." The careless goldsmith was in fact suddenly seized by pains so violent that he thought himself dying. The warning was, however, efficacious, and the pyx was soon placed in Gerard's hands.

Toward the close of 1751, Father Cafaro was transferred from Iliceto to Caposele as Rector. He continued, nevertheless, to direct the beautiful soul of

Gerard, "one of the most privileged," he used to say, "that could possibly be met. His whole life," he added, "was a continual wonder. Our Lord had in all things raised him above his fellow men."

Father Fiocchi succeeded Father Cafaro, and it did not take long for that enlightened religious to divine the treasure he possessed in Gerard. Continual recollection, perfect obedience, heroic abnegation, all proclaimed the high virtue of the young religious; everything in him portrayed the living copy of Jesus Christ. It was under the rectorate of Father Fiocchi that Gerard began that long chain of miracles which procured for him the title of "Thaumaturgus [Wonder-Worker] of the Eighteenth Century."

In consideration of virtue so rare, superiors wrote to St. Alphonsus, the Superior General, asking him to abridge for so holy a novice the time of probation. Toward the middle of January, 1752, Gerard, in consequence, began his second novitiate, and his seraphic ardor redoubled during these six months of solitude.

At last the day of his profession arrived, the great day for which the fervent novice was ardently sighing. On July 16, 1752, the day on which by a happy coincidence the Church was celebrating the feast of Our Lady of Mount Carmel, as well as that of the Most Holy Redeemer, Brother Gerard Majella pronounced the vows of poverty, chastity and obedience, as also the vow and the oath of perseverance in the Congregation of the Most Holy Redeemer. He was thenceforth bound irrevocably to the God of his heart by the golden chains of religion. The lively joy that he experienced could never be expressed. His desires were now fulfilled. He was a Redemptorist, a Redemptorist forever! After offering a thousand thanks to the Blessed Virgin, to whom he confessed himself indebted for his holy vocation, he wrote to St. Alphonsus a letter full of the most filial gratitude.

2. THE SAINTLY REDEMPTORIST

NOW that Gerard belonged entirely to God as a religious, he was going to become in the hand of the Most High an instrument of marvels for the salvation of souls. The first phase of his existence, which we may call his hidden life, was ended; that of his public and apostolic life was about to begin. We shall now see a humble lay brother—knowing at most how to read and write and obliged to appear before the world in order to attend to the needs of the convent—we shall see him, we say, become by his virtues and prodigies a great missionary, a converter of souls, an ideal Redemptorist. So true is it that holiness is preferable to knowledge and talents!

The convent of Iliceto was at this time undergoing the trial of unheard-of poverty. Superiors were forced to implore assistance from benefactors, and Gerard was appointed to this office. He possessed all that was necessary to arouse the generosity of charitable souls: an affable bearing, amiable cordiality, obliging manners and, more than all this, exquisite charity and a heavenly countenance. Everything in him breathed virtue, penance and sanctity.

A lover of the Cross even unto folly, he determined to convert his journeys into constant penance. According to the custom of the country, he went on horseback, but more frequently afoot, graciously offering his horse to any poor man that he happened to meet. His modesty was angelic, and he was careful to keep his eyes cast down. He spread everywhere the good odor of Jesus Christ and the sweetest perfume of virtue.

A disciple of Jesus Crucified, he sought in everything to make of his body a victim of penance. He went around laden with haircloth and little chains. The bare ground was his bed. His scourgings were frequent and even to blood. His life was a perpetual fast, and the little that he took was seasoned with bitter herbs.

Endowed with boundless zeal, "this man of every perfection," as he was called, received with incomparable charity all who came to him, exhorting them to flee from sin, to frequent the Sacraments, to be faithful to the duties of their state. He had received from God an admirable talent for consoling the afflicted, for putting an end to enmities and for reconciling hearts at variance.

The happy families who gave him hospitality never forgot him, but regarded him with a sort of homage. What touched them most was the mortification and piety of the man of God. Once, at the house of Don

Salvadore at Oliveto, they watched him closely and saw that he was all covered with haircloth, that he scourged himself with unheard-of cruelty, that he took scarcely two ounces of nourishment and that he allowed himself at most but two hours of rest, consecrating the remainder of the night to prayer. When he could, he withdrew into some church before the Blessed Sacrament and there remained kneeling long hours, immovable, conversing with his Well-Beloved, and sometimes even ravished in ecstasy.

When the gift of miracles was added to his holy life, we may fancy what prestige the humble Redemptorist would possess over the Italian people. Wherever he went, crowds gathered around him, all eager to see him, hear him and speak to him. It was not only the poor and unlettered that followed him, but the most distinguished men, the noble, the learned, priests, religious—all wished to talk to him, some to consult him, others to excite their fervor, others to disclose to him the sad state of their conscience and to get from him courage to make a good Confession. Even bishops sought his company and his advice.

When the new thaumaturgus was to pass through any place, his renown set the whole country astir. To escape such marks of veneration, he sometimes took back roads. But the inhabitants knew how to frustrate his pious ruses. This happened at Ruvo. The good people had posted sentinels to watch for his coming. What was Brother Gerard's amazement to find a crowd awaiting his arrival to escort him in triumph into the city!

Don Xavier Scoppi, a priest of Melfi, on April 24, 1753, wrote as follows to Father Fiocchi: "Divine Providence has willed that your Brother Gerard should come to Corato for the good of a great number of souls. Thanks to his presence and example, astonishing conversions have been effected. Piety has made sensible progress throughout the entire population. There was about him a continual concourse of gentlemen and persons of distinction. He had only to open his lips to say some words about God in order to convince minds and to fill hearts with compunction. The whole city was stirred by his presence. They praised Gerard to the skies as a Saint come down from Heaven. There was in his language something, I know not what, of the marvelous. Every word was an arrow that went straight to the heart. Several persons have abandoned the world."

We can understand the ascendency of a man clothed with the power of God, who predicted the future, penetrated consciences, cured maladies and, whenever he passed, worked wonders. For the three years that the son of St. Alphonsus journeyed through Pouille, Bari, Basilicata, Avellino and the different Neapolitan provinces, not a day passed without some miracle. The cities of Muro, Corato, Castelgrande, Melfi, Lacedonia, Bisaccia, Calitri, Iliceto, Caposele and a host of towns and villages—even Naples itself, the immense, the beautiful capital—beheld innumerable and most marvelous occurrences, due to the power of Gerard's prayers.

To record them, the historians of the humble brother tell us, an indefatigable chronicler would have been necessary to travel in his footsteps, and even then he would not have succeeded. The cry: "Miracle! Miracle!" resounded everywhere; or again: "The Saint! The Saint!" At Auletta, in consequence of several cures, the servant of God ran and hid himself in a house. But the people followed him, crying: "The Saint! Where is the Saint?" At Naples they pointed him out, saying, "See the Saint!" Such was his renown that the farmers, on seeing him pass, left their work and ran to get his blessing. As Brother Fiore, his faithful companion, kept about a hundred steps ahead of Gerard, it often happened that the people took him for the latter and fell on their knees before him. So he would cry out from a distance, "I am not the Saint, but here he comes."

The liberality of the Faithful, keeping pace with their enthusiasm, had often to be moderated. The women of Muro, according to the expression of Gerard himself, would have willingly despoiled themselves of their gold earrings and the men of their precious effects, had not the good religious checked their generosity.

All these prodigies led to others much greater, namely, to the conversion of sinners and the sanctification of the just. It was not without reason that a certain Bishop said that Gerard's presence in any place was as good as a mission. Thanks to his zeal, parishes were entirely reformed, and convents became for the Divine Spouse a paradise of delights.*

An apostolate so fruitful was likely to excite the rage of Hell, as we may well believe. Two years after the holy brother had made his vows, the blackest calumnies were launched against his reputation. We shall relate them when we touch upon the patience of the servant of God. In the spring of 1754, St. Alphonsus, though without giving credence to the accusation, took occasion from it, nevertheless, to call the brother to Nocera, that he might personally examine his spirit and test his virtue. After keeping him with him for some days, the holy Founder sent him to the convent of Ciorani and ten days later to that of Caposele.

Two months had not passed when the wretched promoter of the calumny, now repentant, confessed her crime. It was at this time that Father Margotta, before going to our convent at Naples, begged St. Alphonsus to give him Gerard as a companion. The servant of God was the same in the capital as he was elsewhere, a holy religious, an apostle, a wonderworker. The crowds that pressed around him and the

---

*As we wish to produce only a popular Life of Brother Gerard, we suppress whatever relates to the spiritual communications he had with religious. There it was that Gerard revealed himself, however, showing his interior life, his wisdom in counsel and the providential mission he had received from God to sanctify monasteries. This part of his life, so interesting to souls consecrated to God, is not suited for the public at large.

marks of veneration of which he was the object were such that Father Margotta judged it prudent to ask the Superior General to remove him temporarily from the great city. Gerard had been there three months and a half.

It was now toward the close of October, 1754. Caposele was assigned him for his residence. This house, of very recent foundation, had for rector Father Cajone. This holy and learned religious confided the care of the convent door to Gerard, and he soon became the happy witness and narrator of the marvels which the admirable brother wrought during the rigorous winter of 1754-1755.

When the excitement produced at Naples by Gerard's sojourn there was somewhat calmed, Father Margotta demanded from Superiors the return of his dear companion. His request was granted. The Father and Gerard went together, first to Calitri, where the latter performed a number of prodigies, and thence to Naples, where his miracles won for him enthusiastic public expressions of tribute on several occasions. His second sojourn in the capital lasted about three months.

In June, 1755, the obedient religious received orders to return to Caposele, where the convent was being built. Its founder, the Archbishop of Conza, eagerly desired to see it finished, but money was lacking. He was obliged to address a circular letter to his diocesans, urging them to concur in a work so eminently useful to the diocese, and he empowered the Redemptorists to receive offerings for the purpose.

No one was more suited for such a mission than Gerard, but unhappily, he was ill. Father Cajone, knowing from experience what obedience could effect in the brother, called him, asked him how he was, then placing his hand on his head without uttering a single word, said interiorly: "In the name of the Most Holy Trinity, I will that your health be restored and that you go on this quest." Gerard was ignorant of the whole affair, but when he saw the rector placing his hand on his head, he said to him: "Your Reverence speaks and speaks not at the same time. You wish me to get well and go on this quest. Ah, I shall get well, and I shall go on the quest!" In fact, Gerard was soon able to start on his mission, thinking less of collecting money, however, than of hastening to the conquest of souls.

He was everywhere received with enthusiasm, and everywhere he gave new proof of the sublime virtues and supernatural gifts with which Heaven had enriched him. These virtues and these gifts we shall now make known to the reader.

—Part Three—

VIRTUES OF
ST. GERARD MAJELLA

1. HIS DESIRE FOR THE
HIGHEST PERFECTION

AFTER the death of Father Cafaro, his first director, Gerard placed himself under the direction
of Father Juvenal, a religious of great virtue. To him
we are indebted for precious documents on the holy
brother's inner life. He soon saw for himself that
Gerard had received from God the gift of reading
hearts, and he had personal experience of it.

One day, he was in great anxiety at the thought
of not being in the grace of God. Just at this time,
Gerard presented himself for Confession. At the end
of it, he said: "Father, rejoice, for you are in the
grace of God. It is the devil who inspires those black
thoughts." The words surprised the priest, but faithful to his practice of humbling the brother whenever an occasion presented itself, he replied shortly:
"You are talking like a madman! You know not what
you are saying," and he dismissed him. But secretly,
Father Juvenal thanked God for having so mar-
velously restored his peace of soul.

What he most admired in his disciple was his perfect obedience, the only security in extraordinary
ways. One day, when Gerard was kept in bed by a
high fever, Father Juvenal ordered him to shake off
his sickness, rise and go to his work. Instantly, the
obedient religious was on his feet and well. On
another occasion, wishing to test him, the priest
ordered him to serve his Mass after having received
Holy Communion. The seraphic brother, knowing
well that love ravished him out of himself every
time he received his Jesus, could not help exclaiming: "But, Father!"

"Do what I tell you," replied the wise director.
The ecstasy did not take place during the Mass, but
immediately afterward.

"To reach perfection," says St. Alphonsus, "two
things are necessary, desire and resolution." These
two secrets of sanctity we find in Gerard. The perfection to which he aspired was not common and
ordinary. He aimed at the highest, hence his heroic
vow to do in everything what was most perfect.
Under pretext of examining whether it was the Spirit
of God that directed him, Father Juvenal ordered
him to put in writing his mortifications, his desires
and his resolutions. Gerard obeyed. Let us give part
of this code of perfection.

"May divine grace be ever in our heart, and may
the Most Blessed Virgin preserve it to us!

"Your Reverence wishes to know my mortifications, my desires, my sentiments, my resolutions,

also the precise meaning of the vow that I have made always to do what is most perfect. I am ready to give an account of all this, in order to walk with more security in the way of salvation.

"*Mortifications*: Every day, I take the discipline, and I wear an iron chain around my loins. On retiring and again on rising, I make a cross on the floor with my tongue. I put bitter herbs in my food at dinner and supper. I wear a heart of iron points on my breast. I chew bitter herbs three times a day. I recite six *Ave Marias*, morning and evening, with my face to the ground.

"On Wednesday, Friday, Saturday and on all vigils, I eat kneeling, and on those days, I leave untasted the fruit at table. On Friday at dinner, I eat less. On Saturday, I fast on bread and water.

"On Wednesday, Friday and Saturday, during the night I wear a large chain and during the day a still larger one around my waist. Day and night I wear one on my arm.

"Every eight days, I take the discipline to blood.

"During novenas, to the aforesaid mortifications, I daily add a discipline, and I take one to blood during the course of the novena, without counting the extraordinary penances for which I ask permission of your Reverence.

"*Desires*: I desire to love my God very much, to live always united to Him, to do everything for Him, to conform in everything to His holy will, to suffer much for Him.

"*Sentiments*: Brother Gerard, do thou resolve to

give thyself to God without reserve. Do not forget that, in order to become a Saint, something more than continual prayer is needed. It is necessary to do the will of God, to consume oneself for God. Behold what God demands of thee. Be a slave neither of the world nor of self. God present—constant union with God—that is sufficient for thee. All that we do for God is a prayer. Some occupy themselves in this, others in that; my only duty is to do the will of God. Nothing costs when we act for God.

"On the 21st of September, I had a better understanding of the following truths: If I were dead six years, what high notions would I have? None. It is a very great pain to suffer and yet not to suffer for God. To endure everything is nothing when we suffer for God. I wish to act upon this earth as if there were but God and myself.

"*Reflections*: If I should be lost, I lose God; and God lost, what remains to me?

"What lively faith I ought to have in the Most Blessed Sacrament of the Altar! Lord, grant that I may bear this in mind!

"*Resolutions*: O my God, only Love of my heart, I abandon myself forever to Thy divine will! In every temptation and trial, I wish to repeat: *Fiat voluntas tua* ["Thy will be done"]. I embrace, I adore Thy divine decrees, and I regard them as so many precious pearls that Thou dost deign to offer me.

"Lord, I wish to do all that Holy Church commands me.

"My God, for love of Thee I will obey all my Superiors as holding Thy place.

"Among all the virtues that are agreeable to Thee, O my God, that which I love best is purity.

"I will speak only in three cases: when there is question of the glory of God, the good of my neighbor or a real necessity.

"In recreation, I will speak only when questioned.

"In temptations to speak against the good pleasure of God, I will say: My God, I love Thee!

"I will say neither good nor evil of myself, but I will act as if I were not.

"I will never excuse myself, even if I have the best reasons for doing so, provided my silence cause no offense to God and no prejudice to my neighbor.

"I will never reply to him who reprimands me, unless he expects it of me.

"I will be an enemy of every irregularity.

"I will never accuse others, nor speak of their defects, not even in jest.

"I will always excuse my neighbor, beholding in him Jesus Christ Himself, who in spite of His innocence, was accused by the Jews. I will always defend the absent.

"I will report whoever speaks ill of his neighbor.

"I will act in such a manner as not to give others an occasion of impatience.

"If anyone commits a fault, I will take care not to tax him with it in the presence of others; but I will do it in private, in charity and in a low voice.

"Should a Father or a brother have need of help,

I will leave everything to assist him, unless obedience ordains otherwise.

"I will, with permission, visit the sick several times in the day.

"I will never interfere in the affairs of others.

"In every employment in which I have to help others, I will, without reply, obey him who presides.

"In the common duties, such as sweeping, carrying loads, etc., my rules shall be never to take the best place nor the best tools, but I will yield to others what is most convenient, taking for myself whatever God will leave for me. In this way, everyone will be satisfied, and I among the rest.

"In moments of excitement, I will not act contrary to reason, but before acting, I will wait till calm returns.

"My great resolution is to give myself entirely to God. Therefore, I will have always before my eyes the three words: 'deaf, dumb, blind.'

"These words: *I will* and *I will not*, shall never cross my lips. Thy will, O my God, and not mine!

"To do the will of God, I must renounce my own. Yes, God alone, and if I wish but God alone, I must renounce everything that is not God.

"In nothing will I seek my own interests.

"During the hours of silence, I will meditate on the Passion of Jesus Christ and the Sorrows of Mary."

We shall now treat in detail the virtues of this holy religious. They will convince us that he was "an angel in the flesh, a seraph of love for God and neighbor, a model of all virtues, the Saint of obedience, a prodigy of penance, a true mirror of Christian perfection, the ideal of humility, a hunter of souls, the father of the poor, a man entirely of God, a holy wonder-worker, a Saint by excellence." All these high praises have been bestowed upon him by his contemporaries, as the Cause of his Beatification testifies.

2. HIS FAITH

ACCORDING to the teaching of the Holy Council of Trent, faith is the foundation, the root and the source of justification and of every supernatural virtue. If Brother Gerard arrived at so eminent a perfection, it was all due to his lively, ardent and heroic faith. Its best eulogy is contained in the words of the great servant of God. "Faith is my life," he wrote, "and life for me is faith. O God! what man could live without holy Faith? As for me, would that I could cry out continually and make resound over all the earth: 'Live the holy Faith of our God!'"

Thence sprang his perfect submission to Holy Church. "Lord," he would say, "I wish to do all that Holy Church, my Mother, orders me to do"; thence, this sentiment that he so loved to repeat, that he would give his life a thousand times in defense of revealed truths; thence that ardent desire for martyrdom, which he offered to God every morning when renewing his holy vows; thence that truly profound knowledge of religion which he had, although with no other instruction than that received in primary schools; thence, finally, that supernatural spirit which vivified his whole life.

The spirit of faith showed him Jesus Christ in the priest, in his Superiors, in his confreres, in the poor, in the sick.

"When receiving the benediction of my Superior," he said, "I think it is Jesus Christ Himself who is giving it to me."

"I will obey my Superior as I would the Person of Jesus Christ."

"I will take care to excuse all my fellow religious, seeing in them Our Lord Jesus Christ, whom the Jews accused in spite of His innocence."

"I will have the most profound veneration for priests, seeing in them Jesus Christ Himself."

Everything that recalled the mysteries of our Holy Faith aroused the devotion of the saintly Redemptorist in the highest degree. "I will recite a *Gloria Patri*," he said, "whenever I see a Crucifix or any image representing one of the Three Divine Persons, or when I hear Them named, and at the beginning and at the end of each of my actions, besides." It is to the liveliness of his faith, which in some way rendered visible to him the great invisible God, that we must attribute his frequent ecstasies. He could not—without being ravished out of himself—contemplate the sublime mysteries, such as the Most Holy Trinity, the Incarnation, the Passion, the Blessed Sacrament.

In 1753, the eve of the feast of the Most Blessed Trinity, Gerard was called to the convent of San Salvatore at Foggia to console a sick religious. Just as he had finished, they began to chant in choir the first Vespers of the feast. Hardly had he heard the words, *Gloria Tibi, Trinitas*—"Glory to Thee, O Trinity!" than he was seized with a transport of love. Ravished in ecstasy, he crossed the cloister with arrow-like speed, repeating these words of St. Paul: "O the depth of the riches of the wisdom and of the knowledge of God! How incomprehensible are His judgments, and how unsearchable are His ways!" At the end of the Office, seeing the nuns pause to gaze with emotion at his state of ecstatic joy, he exclaimed with holy enthusiasm: "O Sisters, let us love God! O Sisters, let us love God!" Then suddenly raising his eyes toward Heaven, he was elevated to a considerable height in the air.

It was above all in his office of sacristan that Gerard showed forth his lively faith. Who could express the joy that he experienced when ornamenting the altars, the statues, the crib and the repository! To labor for Jesus, so near to Jesus, under the eyes of Jesus—that was for him a foretaste of Paradise.

His ardent faith urged him to pass every leisure moment before the Blessed Sacrament. What piety, what respect at the foot of the holy altar! One would have thought him a seraph in adoration before the throne of God.

The Blessed Sacrament was the magnet that attracted his heart. When It was exposed for the veneration of the Faithful, he was out of himself, and sometimes he fell swooning before the people. It was a beautiful sight to witness his struggles at times between his love for Jesus Christ and his respect for obedience. Father Tannoia relates that one day, hidden in a corner of the church, he saw the angelic religious pass by and kneel before the sacred Tabernacle. Then he tried to rise. At last, as if detained by an invisible force, he exclaimed: "Ah, Lord, let me go, for I have to do my work!" And he ran off hastily, as if tearing himself away from sweet converse with his God.

What did he not do to excite in the Faithful ardent faith in this Mystery of Love! The sight of the Tabernacle with but few adorers was a real suffering to him. Thanks to his zeal and example, the daily visit to the Blessed Sacrament was established in many localities. He went so far as even to promote frequent Communion, not only in certain chosen souls, but in whole families and districts. It was said of him that he knew how to attract more souls to the Holy Table than did a hundred preachers.

His lively faith was excited also at the remembrance of the Passion, and the Crucifix was the object of his continual contemplation. Jesus Crucified absorbed all his thoughts, and the sight of Him on the Cross often threw him into ecstasy. Several young students had come to make a retreat in our convent of Iliceto, and the pious sacristan was charged with attending to their meals. In the refectory hung a picture of the *Ecce Homo* [Christ before Pilate]. In the middle of his work, Gerard, a fork in one hand, a napkin in the other, raised his eyes, and seeing the Man of Sorrows, he paused immovable, his eyes fixed on the holy picture. A brother who happened to be passing at the time called him, but without effect. Soon others gathered, and lastly, the Father Rector appeared on the scene. Confident that Gerard was in ecstasy, he ordered him to return to his senses, and immediately the rapture ceased.

It is to the lively faith of this good brother that we must attribute that multitude of miracles which he wrought in the name of the Most Holy Trinity and by the Sign of the Cross. Has not Jesus Christ said in the Gospel: "All things are possible to him that believeth"? (*Mark* 9:22). He who has faith is master of the world. God seems to subject His almighty power to the man of faith.

"Courage," said the servant of God one day to a sick person, while making on him the Sign of the Cross, "Courage! Rise and come with me to the church to Confession." And the sick man was cured at the same instant. In the same way and instantaneously he restored health to a sick lay sister of San Salvatore, Foggia, at the moment she seemed about to expire. It was by the Sign of the Cross that he gave perfect health to a young girl whom all the efforts of medical art had failed to cure. "Be cured," he said to her, and at the word, she was cured. And how many times this prodigy was repeated!

He had the same faith in the power of holy water, which he made use of to strengthen himself against

the assaults of Hell. When the demons had bruised
him all over with blows, a few drops of holy water
instantaneously cured his wounds. The relics of the
Saints were likewise the objects of his faith. He often
made use of the dust from the tomb of St. Teresa
to cure the sick or to prevent accidents.

3. HIS HOPE

HOPE proceeds from faith as the stem from the
root. The deeper the root of faith, the stronger
will be the stem of hope. A soul so filled with faith
as was Gerard must necessarily be animated with
great hope and a truly filial confidence in God. Once
he was asked whether he had certain hope of his
eternal salvation. "Yes," he answered, "since it was
to obtain this favor for me that Jesus Christ came
upon earth."

He hoped firmly, not only to attain Paradise, but
even the highest sanctity. Thus this word so often
on his lips: "I wish to become a Saint." At no period
of his life did he cease to pursue this noble end so
worthy of a generous soul. He aimed at it with coura-
geous ardor and most admirable perseverance. He
omitted no proper means for reaching perfection:
continual prayer, frequent Communions, cruel
penances, a passionate seeking after suffering, the
perfect renunciation of all earthly things and unreserved surrender of self to Jesus and Mary. In the
farewell letter that he addressed to his mother when
he withdrew from her maternal care in order to

embrace the religious life, we read these words: "I am going to become a Saint." In spite of the thousand difficulties raised by superiors against his entrance into the Congregation, he hoped against all hope. He knew by the constancy of his prayers how to gain the favor which seemed irrevocably denied.

Once admitted, Gerard put no bounds to his desires for spiritual advancement. In his resolutions, we find them thus expressed: "The chance to become a Saint is offered me only once. If I do not profit by it, it is gone forever. Since I can have only once the good fortune to become a Saint, what shall hinder me from laboring for that end? I have every opportunity to sanctify myself. Yes, I will be a Saint."

Knowing that the work of sanctification demands both the help of God and the cooperation of man, Gerard formed strong and serious resolutions, but he counted only on the grace of God to observe them faithfully. "Never have I depended on myself, never will I depend on myself! Knowing my profound misery, I would never depend on myself. If I ever did so, I was certainly out of my mind. In God, in God alone do I confide, do I hope. I have placed my whole life in His hands, that He may do with me what He pleases. And although I live, yet I am without life, since my life is God. In Him alone I rest. From Him alone I expect the help necessary to carry out my resolutions."

To obtain this fidelity, the humble religious offered to God this prayer: "Grant, O Lord, that I may be faithful to my resolutions. Alas! I cannot depend upon myself, incapable as I am of fulfilling the least commitment. But I confide in Thee alone, Who art Goodness and infinite Mercy and Who cannot fail in Thy promises. O Supreme Goodness, when I failed, the failure was on my side! Henceforth I desire Thee to act in me. Grant, O Lord, that I may keep my resolutions exactly and without fault. I firmly hope for this from Thee, O Thou inexhaustible Treasure!"

The saintly brother also confided in the help of the Blessed Virgin, the Angels and the Saints. "And thou, Immaculate Virgin Mary, my only joy, be thou my protectress and my consoler! Be ever my advocate with God, that I may put into practice my good resolutions."

"I turn to you, O blessed inhabitants of Heaven, and I beg you to be my advocates with our Creator. It is in your presence that I write these lines. Deign to read them from the heights of Heaven, and pray the Divine Majesty that I may be faithful to them. May your prayers be efficacious! It is in your presence that I make these promises to God and to Mary. I beg my holy patronesses, Teresa, Mary Magdalen of Pazzi and Agnes to give me their special and continual help."

When the terrible trials to which he was subjected arose, Gerard showed that his hope in God was as unshaken as the rock lashed by the tempest. Like all the Saints, he had to pass through the crucible of tribulations, aridity, agony and terror. We tremble when we think of the combats against the rage of Hell that he had to sustain, the bitterness he had to experience when the most atrocious calumnies were launched against him, and the unceasing violence he had to do himself, to lead (until death) a life so mortified, so penitential. Supported by God, he never yielded to discouragement. With St. Paul, he exclaimed: "I can do all things in Him who strengtheneth me." (*Phil.* 4:13).

God himself wished to rejoice in the beautiful spectacle of this heroic virtue by delivering His servant to unspeakable abandonment. Yes, this pure soul, so rich in heavenly gifts, so favored with ecstasies and seraphic ardors, had to sustain a terrible struggle against despair and the fear of being abandoned by God. He himself reveals this painful martyrdom in his letters, from which we extract the following passages: "Divine Justice tortures me in such a way that I think no one has more to suffer. May the will of God be eternally blessed! What makes me tremble and causes me the greatest fright is the thought that I shall not persevere. I behold myself in total weakness, plunged in an ocean of confusion and suspended, as it were, above the abyss of despair. It seems to me that there is no longer any God for me, that His divine mercies are exhausted and that only His Justice is hanging over my head. Behold the unhappy state in which I am! I am nailed to the Cross. Have compassion on my agony. My tears almost prevent my writing these lines. My sufferings are so bitter that they make me experience the agonies of death."

In the midst of these waves of affliction, the holy Redemptorist supported himself by heroic confidence. "May God be forever blessed for the graces with which He has laden me! Instead of allowing me to die under His blows, He sustains me that I may live. If He sends me these trials, it is only that I may imitate the Divine Redeemer. He is my Master; I am His disciple. I must, then, learn to walk in His footsteps. With Him I am nailed to the Cross, plunged in affliction, a prey to untold sufferings. I feel as if a lance were piercing me with a death-blow. Not to resist the designs of my Saviour, who wants to nail me like Himself to the Cross, I incline my head and repeat: 'Yes, it is the will of God whom I love. Yes, I accept, I embrace it.' " These words recall the utterance of the Royal Prophet: "Though He should slay me, yet will I hope in Him."

God never abandons His servants in their afflictions, and therefore He had in reserve for Gerard unheard-of consolations. There was at Iliceto a young religious who, by his innocence and interior life, was called by his companions another St. Aloysius Gonzaga. His name was Dominic Blasucci. Struck one day by Gerard's pallor, he asked him the cause. The Saint revealed to him in all simplicity the agony and despair that tortured his soul and begged the young ecclesiastic to come to his aid. For answer, Dominic made the Sign of the Cross on his heart. At that instant, the trial vanished, giving place to the sweetest consolations.

Gerard's sublime confidence extended even to the

necessities of life. He lived without solicitude, knowing that no father is so good as God is to His children. The Redemptorists owned at Naples a house given to St. Alphonsus by his brother, Don Hercules di Liguori. It was in this house that Father Margotta and Brother Gerard, his companion, worked out their sanctification by their piety and most austere penances. There was between these two souls a holy emulation as to which should practice the greater mortification. Both were constantly laden with haircloth and chains. The bare ground was their bed, and daily they scourged themselves to blood. The Superior never troubled himself about food, and Gerard thought still less about it. One day, on returning to the convent, the Father asked Gerard what he had prepared for the next meal. "All that you ordered," answered the brother smiling, "and nothing more." Needless to say, nothing was prepared.

The poverty of the convent at Naples was great. This want of necessities distressed the holy brother, not on his own account (admirable lover of holy poverty that he was!), but on account of the poor to whom he had nothing to give.

Brother Francis Tartaglione, who was on a visit of some days at this convent, gave his confrere some money to buy food and prepare a repast. Gerard went out to make his purchase. On his way, he met a peddler selling flints and lighters. The poor fellow asked alms of the brother, saying that he was dying of hunger. Filled with compassion, Gerard forgot his bread and fish and gave in exchange for the peddler's wares all the money that he had just received. Meantime, Brother Francis, who had had certain errands to perform, returned to the convent and asked Gerard what he had prepared for dinner. Gerard's only answer was to embrace him joyously, saying: "Why so much solicitude? God alone and nothing more!"

"Oh, that's all very well," returned the brother, "but we must think a little about eating." Seeing on the table the flints and lighters, he asked: "What's all this?"

"My dear Brother," answered Gerard, "that may be of use to us some day. I must tell you candidly that I met a poor man selling them. He was dying of hunger, so I could not help buying them from him with the money you gave me." This explanation, as we may readily understand, was not a most pleasing one to Brother Francis, but admiring the charity of his confrere, he hid his chagrin.

While this was going on, the Superior entered, and Gerard hastened to tell him of his having presumed his permission to give the alms. "But we, what have we to eat?" asked the Father, smiling. "God will provide, dear Father," was the reply. And indeed, toward the dinner hour, the bell rang. It was a servant bringing to the community a basket full of provisions from his mistress.

The marvels of Gerard's life could have no other source than his own great confidence in God. Money failed during the building of the convent of Caposele. The Father Rector imparted the fact to Gerard, who advised him to call on the King of kings. Father Cajone, accordingly, drew up a formal petition to Almighty God and gave it to the saintly brother to present to His Divine Majesty. Without a second thought, Gerard went straight to the church, laid the letter on the altar and, with the holy audacity of faith, knocked at the door of the Tabernacle, saying, "Here, O Lord, is our petition. Thou must answer it."

It was Friday, and the money had to be forthcoming by the next day, Saturday, to pay the workmen. Gerard passed that night before the Blessed Sacrament, begging Jesus Christ to come to the aid of the community. At daybreak, he knocked again at the door of the Tabernacle to commend his request to Our Lord. At that same instant, a ring at the bell was heard. Gerard ran to the door and there found two bags of money. It was the Divine Master's answer to the prayer of His well-beloved servant.

Our Saint loved to say that nothing could possibly be impossible to those who hope in God. Thence came those miraculous cures so ordinary with him.

A poor consumptive of Iliceto was in a state of despair. "The lungs are entirely gone," declared the doctor, "and it is not in my power to replace them." Gerard visited the sick man and gave him some hope of recovery. "No!" exclaimed the doctor, "he cannot get well. His lungs are too far gone."

"But God," replied the holy brother—"is He not powerful enough to make new lungs? May it please Him to work this miracle in order to inspire the Faithful to put their trust in Him and in Him alone!"

With these words, and promising the sick man to pray for him, the brother left. Some days after, the man was perfectly cured.

This confidence in God, which the holy Redemptorist possessed in so high a degree, he knew how to breathe into others, even the most despairing sinners. One day, as he was going to the city of Saint Agatha, an interior voice told him that he would meet a great sinner. Soon, in fact, a man of gloomy and melancholy aspect came along. "Whither are you going, my friend?" inquired Gerard kindly.

"What is that to you? Leave me in peace," responded the wayfarer fiercely.

"Who knows?" returned the servant of God. "Perhaps I might be of use to you."

"I go my way, you go yours!" exclaimed the wretch angrily. "Do not trouble me."

"I know you are in despair," replied the good brother. "I know that you are on the point of delivering your soul to the demon. Have confidence. God has sent me this way expressly for you."

On hearing these words, the unhappy man burst into tears. Hope sprang up in his heart, and he revealed to Gerard the cause of his misery. The latter consoled and encouraged him, advising him to make a good Confession to Father Fiocchi. Such was the fervor of his conversion that they kept him as a servant in the convent. Several years later, he consecrated himself to the service of the sick in a hospital at Naples. His name was Francis Teta.

4. HIS LOVE FOR GOD

THE love of God, says St. John, consists in the observance of His Commandments. Hence it follows that the more faithful a soul is to the divine law, the more carefully it shuns the least violation of that law, the more it loves God. This principle affords us the true measure of Brother Gerard's love for his God. We know from the unanimous testimony of his directors that this angelic soul committed not only no mortal sin, but even—unheard-of prodigy(!)—no deliberate venial fault. Though sounding the depths of his pure conscience, they could never find in his whole life sufficient matter for sacramental absolution. Interior purity was so manifest in the whole person of this privileged just man, in his countenance, his look, his words, his bearing, his gestures, his whole deportment, that his contemporaries went so far as to say that he had not sinned in Adam, or that he had no other sin than the Original Stain, which Baptism had removed. Free from all sin and from every obstacle to divine love, the beautiful soul of Gerard could soar toward its God, light as a flame, and approach Him like the Seraphim. And that is what he did.

Man's heart is created to love God. Gerard well understood this. He desired to love Him, to love Him much, to love Him as the Seraphim. Oh, noble ambition, which shone forth in this beautiful act of love: "My God, I make the intention of offering to Thee as many acts of love as the Blessed Virgin, all the

Blessed spirits, as also all the Faithful on earth have ever produced. I desire to love Thee as much as Jesus Christ loves Thee. I wish to renew these acts at every pulsation of my heart." These were his habitual sentiments. He wrote to a religious of eminent holiness, Mother Maria Celestia Crostarosa, Superioress of the Sisters of San Salvatore at Foggia: "I desire to love God. I desire to remain always near to God. I desire to do all things through love of my God." The religious of San Salvatore tell us that, when Brother Gerard opened his mouth, his heart was like a volcano of love. His inflamed countenance was like that of an Angel descending to speak among men.

One day, he laid his hand on the breast of a servant of the Bishop of Melfi and, in the accents of a Seraph, repeated these burning words: "Let us love God! Let us love God!" While pronouncing them, his countenance appeared radiant. In a visit made to the Canon Rossi at Melfi, the latter turned the conversation upon the perfections of God. Gerard at once fell into ecstasy. His face was as if on fire, a heavenly light shone on his forehead, and his heart beat violently, as if about to leap from his breast. The Canon, divining his state, bathed his breast with water and thus extinguished the divine flames.

The sight of holy images, paintings and pious statues, which others regard with indifference, inflamed the heart of the holy Redemptorist. During his stay at Naples, he saw one day a carving of the Crucifix and the *Ecce Homo* [Christ before Pilate].

He immediately showed an eager desire to learn the art in order to propagate the image of Him whom he loved. The artist offered to give him lessons, and the servant of God soon became an able carver. Many of his works are still preserved with respect. They are so expressive, say the owners, "that we cannot look upon them without being touched."

We may say that Gerard was smitten with love for Jesus Crucified—even to madness. He never interrupted his meditations on the sufferings of his Divine Master. He wished to become himself a living image of Jesus scourged, crowned with thorns and nailed to the Cross.

On the grounds of the convent of Iliceto there was a grotto once sanctified by the presence of Blessed Felix di Corsano. It was there that Gerard retired to practice the most cruel penances. His confidant was a young postulant named Andrew Longarelli, to whom, in spite of his lively repugnance, he gave the order to fulfill toward him the role of executioner. The lover of the Cross first had himself fastened to a stake, his hands bound, like the Saviour at the pillar. Then with cords wet and twisted, he was scourged until the blood flowed on all sides. Placing on his head a crown of thorns, he ordered Andrew to force it down with the blows of a reed, which made the blood flow abundantly. He went even so far as to have himself attached with cords to a cross, earnestly begging his young executioner, whose tears of commiseration were flowing, to stretch his arms and legs as had been done to Our Lord. These bloody scenes took place during Gerard's first novitiate and ceased only at the prohibition of Father Cafaro.

During his second novitiate, Gerard was able to obtain permission to follow his attraction for these extraordinary mortifications. This time it was the tailor Francis Teta who was to act as executioner, and when he refused to discharge the office, the servant of God would say to him in a supplicating voice: "Oh, strike me! I command you in obedience, strike me!" One day, after having himself fastened to a large cross and raised in the air, the weight of his body and the countershock caused him the most acute suffering. At the same time, he had a crown of thorns forced into his head by heavy blows from a reed. These holy follies of love, of which we have already seen examples, ceased only at the voice of obedience.

During Mass, Gerard seemed to be one of the Seraphim present at the scene on Calvary. Famishing for the Eucharistic Bread, his soul was in torture when deprived of It, and so he had permission to communicate every morning. "Ordinarily," he wrote in his resolutions, "I will not ask permission on the evening before to communicate the next day. I will ask it only as I am going to church, in order to keep myself always ready for Communion. If the permission is refused, I will make a Spiritual Communion when the priest receives the Sacred Host. My thanksgiving will last from the moment of Communion till noon, and my preparation for the morrow from noon till six o'clock in the evening."

Once, when at Atella, at the house of his friend Canon Bozzio, through humility he dared not approach the Holy Table. That whole day he experienced so great a hunger for the Heavenly Bread that he went out into the fields to try to distract himself from his devouring desire for his Well-Beloved.

After communicating his seraphic ardor elevated him to a kind of ecstasy, which made him forget the things of this world. One day when he had the care of the kitchen, after having received his God, he retired before a large Crucifix to make his thanksgiving. At the dinner hour, nothing had been prepared. Gerard was sought everywhere and at last they found him, entirely absorbed in God, his face inflamed. "What have you been doing?" said a brother to him. "There is nothing ready for dinner." "Man of little faith," responded the holy Redemptorist, "what have the Angels been doing?" The Angels had indeed been at his service, for at the usual hour a meal was served as on the best of days.

Gerard's love for the Blessed Sacrament chained him to the foot of the altar. The Holy Place had for him such charms that only his duties were capable of drawing him away from it. After having passed there a great part of the day, he spent most of the night in the same place. He had to make painful efforts to tear himself away from our holy Tabernacles. We may say that Jesus had conquered the heart of Gerard and that Gerard had given it to

Him without reserve. Jesus and Gerard formed but
one heart and one soul, so strictly had grace and
love bound them together. There were between them,
therefore, relations of astonishing familiarity.

One day, the superior of Caposele perceived the
brother smiling when passing before the Blessed
Sacrament, and he asked him the reason. From the
ingenuous answer of the Saint, he understood that
another exchange of words holily familiar had taken
place between the Saviour and him, such as we have
recorded at the beginning of this work. Dr.
Santorelli* asked him once why he passed so quickly
before the main altar. "What would you have me
do?" replied Gerard. "This good Saviour so often
stops me!" He had hardly uttered the words when,
with a great cry, he fell into ecstasy. Next day, meeting the doctor, who was smiling, he said, "Did I not
tell you? You have seen how this good Master takes
me by surprise."

There are few souls who enter further into the
Heart of Jesus than did this admirable brother. The
name alone of the Heart of Jesus made him thrill
with joy. He wrote once to Mother Maria of Jesus,
Superioress of the Carmel of Ripacandida: "You can
speak to me no longer, you say, except in the Heart

---

*The physician, Dr. Santorelli, of whom frequent mention is
made in this Life, was the friend and confidant of Brother
Gerard. He was a man of great piety. He communicated daily,
consecrated several hours in the day to prayer, assiduously frequented our church and practiced the most austere penance.

of Jesus. Oh, if you knew the happiness I have experienced on hearing such words!" It was in that Heart that he saw the friends in whom he was interested. "I declare in all truth," he said to the same religious, "I have not once conversed with the Lord without seeing you in His Sacred Heart." This Heart he offered to God as the only Gift worthy of His Majesty. "And then," he goes on to say, "I offer this most holy Heart to God for you." In this Heart he made his perpetual abode. "Let us remain always in the Sacred Heart of Jesus," he would say, and he recommended to holy souls to establish their dwelling in It. "Oh, how I desire that you and all your dear sisters would dwell forever in the pierced Heart of Jesus! In this Heart is found all sweetness, and there is rest."

In his seraphic love, he could not comprehend how man could offend the Infinite Majesty. He had vowed implacable hatred toward sin, which he looked upon as the executioner of Jesus. From hence came his ardent zeal to extirpate sin from souls. But among sins there was none so supremely revolting to his heart as sacrilegious Communion.

The Bishop of Lacedonia had sent to Iliceto a hardened sinner to make there the exercises of a retreat. On the day of Communion, Gerard met him. "Where are you going?" he asked.

"I am going to Communion," was the answer.

"To Communion!" exclaimed the brother, beside himself. "What! You go to Communion! And despite this sin, and that other sin which you have not confessed! Go, go quickly and make a good Confession if you do not want the earth to swallow you."

These inspired words led the sinner to enter into himself. He made a sincere Confession and returned to his own city transformed into a new man. But his conversion was not lasting. The following year, the relapsed sinner, now worse than before, presented himself anew to make the retreat. Again Gerard inquired as to the state of his soul.

"All is well," answered the hypocrite. "I have not relapsed into my old sins."

The brother, who read the contrary in his poor soul, took a crucifix: "What!" he cried in a tone of indignation, "you have had the heart thus to offend your God! What! you have not relapsed? Look at this crucifix! Who has made these wounds on Jesus Christ? And who but you has made this blood flow from the veins of the Saviour?" At the same moment, the blood began to flow from the hands and feet of the crucifix.

"What injury has your God done you?" pursued Gerard. "For you He willed to be born a little Child in a crib; for you He was laid upon straw." At these words, the Child Jesus appeared in the hands of the servant of God, who finished by saying: "What! you dare thus to mock your God! Ah! know that this is never done with impunity. He is patient, but He chastises in the end." And now appeared a frightful demon to drag the hardened wretch into Hell. "Begone, vile beast!" cried Gerard, and the demon instantly disappeared. Needless to say, the sinner was sincere this time in his conversion and became a model of virtue.

5. HIS DEVOTION TO THE MOST BLESSED VIRGIN MARY

GERARD would not have been a worthy son of St. Alphonsus if he had had only an ordinary devotion to the Blessed Virgin. From his infancy he had given her his heart, and until his last sigh he faithfully guarded it for her. The Blessed Virgin had so ravished his heart that it would be difficult to find, even among the Saints most devoted to Mary, a servant who loved her more passionately. This holy passion became still more ardent when the good young man had the happiness of seeing himself a Redemptorist. The Queen of Heaven hastened to recompense him for his love by giving him a wonderful knowledge of her greatness. We shall see, further on, the heavenly illumination given him on the subject of the grand mystery of the Incarnation and the sublimity of the divine Maternity. Mary, Mother of God–this thought revealed to him a whole world of marvels!

Considering that he owed to this loving Queen the great grace of his vocation, he knew not in what terms to testify his gratitude. The name alone of Mary was sufficient to make him fall into ecstasy, and the sight of her image threw him into the sweetest transports. He wished to be all to Mary, as he

wished to be all to Jesus, that he might go by her
to Jesus. He desired to breathe but for Mary. We
read in his rule of life that he made the intention of
offering to her as many acts of love as all the just
on earth and all the Blessed in Heaven had ever
offered her. He went so far as to desire to love her
as much as Our Lord Himself had loved her. And
these acts of love he wished, as he said, to repeat
at every pulsation of his heart.

The Redemptorists are bound by rule to recite five
decades of the Rosary, to make a visit to the Blessed
Virgin and to say a certain number of *Ave Marias*
[Hail Marys] every day. They fast, also, on the eves
of Mary's feasts and abstain from meat every
Saturday in the year [Saturday being Mary's special
day of the week]. Gerard was not satisfied with these
marks of filial love. "Before and after every meal,"
he wrote in his resolutions, "I will recite three *Ave
Marias*; when taking a drink of water, one *Ave
Maria*; every time the clock strikes, one *Ave Maria*."
Still more, he recited a *Gloria Patri* [Glory be to
the Father] every time he saw an image of the
Blessed Virgin, whenever he heard her name pronounced, and at the beginning and end of every
action. He constantly wore a Rosary around his neck
as a sign that he lived in the blessed chains of Mary.

Every Saturday he fasted on bread and water and
took the discipline to blood. During the novenas, he
observed a severe abstinence and imposed upon himself cruel mortifications and other good works.
When he was able, he passed the night before

Mary's feasts at the foot of her shrine. His devotion to the Immaculate Conception was incomparable. How often he was rapt in ecstasy before her image! It was at her feet that he publicly made the vow of virginity in the Cathedral of Muro, a vow which he had probably made in his heart many years before. It was without doubt in recompense for this special devotion that he was received, in spite of all human obstacles, into an Institute of which the Blessed Virgin is the great patroness. His love for the Passion of Jesus Christ led him also to honor especially the Mother of Sorrows. This favorite of Jesus Crucified ever stood, like St. John, by Mary's side at the foot of the Cross.

One day, Doctor Santorelli asked him whether he loved the Blessed Virgin. "My dear Doctor," he answered, his countenance in a glow, "you torture me. What a question!" And he ran off quickly to hide the fire that consumed him.

Once, at the house of Father Sabatelli of Foggia, surrounded by priests and others, he began to speak of the love borne us by the Divine Mother. The thought excited in him so great a fervor of love that he fell into an ecstasy, which lasted three hours.

On another occasion, being at the home of the Scoppi family at Melfi, he happened to cast his eyes on a picture of the Blessed Virgin. Instantly, he was so inflamed with love that he was raised like a feather from the ground to a level with the picture. Kissing it, he exclaimed, "O Donna Anna, what a beautiful Virgin you have!" Donna Anna Scoppi, the lady of the house, was so overcome that she fainted.

The lover of the Mother of God constituted himself her apostle. Wherever he went, he spoke of his good Mother with such zeal that he inflamed all hearts. The nuns of Corato used to say that when Brother Gerard spoke of the most Blessed Virgin— and he did so very often—it was with such fervor and tenderness that he communicated his own love to all who heard him, giving them some idea of what the Seraphim must be.

The duty of sacristan, confided to him at Iliceto, was particularly dear to his heart, as it offered him an occasion of honoring his beloved Lady.

On the approach of her festivals, he could be seen full of solicitude, ornamenting her altar, arranging the most beautiful flowers and the most brilliant lights, organizing the processions that were to be made and trying to enhance the grandeur of the occasion with fireworks and the discharge of guns. He loved dearly to spread devotion to the Rosary and the Scapular, and it was without doubt in recompense for this zeal that at the moment of death, his face all aglow, he suddenly exclaimed to his infirmarian, "Look, Brother, look! The Scapulars!"

Mary loves those that love her, and she is never surpassed in love by anyone. Consequently, she had with this child of predilection incomparable communications. One night, in our church of Iliceto, she appeared to him resplendent with beauty and lavished on him marks of the most maternal tenderness.

Another most touching scene took place at Melfi. Gerard, with some priests and laymen, was visiting the picture gallery of the Canon Capucci. Suddenly, his eyes were fixed on a painting of the Virgin. At the same instant, he was elevated to the height of the holy picture, and seizing it in transport, he covered it with pious kisses, exclaiming, "How beautiful she is! How beautiful she is! See how beautiful she is!" The witnesses of this scene were moved even to tears.

6. HIS DEVOTION TO THE SAINTS AND ANGELS, AND PARTICULARLY TO ST. MICHAEL

A CHILD of Heaven rather than of earth, Gerard had chosen his intimate friends from among the Angels and the Saints. Besides the Twelve Apostles, he daily honored his Guardian Angel, St. Joseph, Sts. Joachim and Anne, St. John the Baptist, St. Bernard, St. Philip Neri, St. Mary Magdalen the Penitent, St. Francis Xavier, St. Teresa, St. Francis of Assisi, St. Felix Cantalice, the Forty Martyrs, the Saint of his birthday, and also the Saint of the day on which he was to die. But nothing equalled his tender devotion to the Archangel Michael, who lavished on him so many privileged favors during the course of his life.

The young Redemptorists who studied theology at Iliceto obtained permission to visit, during the vacation of September, 1753, the celebrated grotto of the Archangel on Mount Gargano, and Brother Gerard was appointed to take charge of them. It was a great satisfaction for this pious brother to be able to present in person his homage to his celestial protector. Our pilgrims received only twenty carlins (12 francs, 50 centimes; or less than 3 dollars) for the journey, although they numbered not fewer than twelve persons and the pilgrimage would last nine days. To the students' remarks on the smallness of the sum, Gerard replied, "God will provide." A hermit undertook to accompany them with two rented donkeys. On passing by Foggia, they went to venerate the miraculous picture of the Blessed Virgin, before which St. Alphonsus had been twice publicly favored with an ecstasy.

A religious of the Annunciation wished to take advantage of the saintly brother's presence to confer with him on the state of her soul, but what was her surprise when the man of God told her to prepare to quit this earth at once. This news was so much the more unexpected to the sister since she was in the flower of her age and in full health. The sequel, however, soon proved the truth of the prophecy.

During all this journey, Gerard did not cease to show his confidence in God. Seeing the young people worn out by fatigue, he rented a wagon.

"But how shall we pay for it?" they said to him.

"God will provide," responded the holy brother.

And now the two donkeys refused to go forward. The hermit, losing patience, wanted to leave them at a public-house till their return. "I take upon myself to make them go on," said Gerard, smiling, and touching them with his stick, he said, "In the name of the Most Holy Trinity, go on! I order you!" The poor beasts immediately stepped out at a quick pace, which they kept up the rest of the journey.

When they reached Manfredonia, the purse contained only one franc. Far from losing confidence, Gerard, seeing a beautiful bouquet for sale, bought it, took it to the church and, placing it before the Tabernacle, said to Jesus Christ: "See, Lord, I have been thinking of Thee. Do Thou deign to think of my little family."

The chaplain of the chateau, a witness of this act of devotion, called the devout servant of Christ and begged him and all his companions to accept his hospitality. "May God be your reward," replied Gerard, "but there are too many of us!"

"Never mind that. Let all come. I regret only one thing, and that is, that my mother, who has been ill for two months, cannot receive you as you deserve."

"There is a remedy for her sickness," replied the brother. "Make a Sign of the Cross on the forehead of the sick woman, and she will be cured." And indeed, hardly had she been signed with the Cross when she was perfectly restored.

The devotion of the holy Redemptorist to the Blessed Sacrament made such an impression on another priest of the place that he presented him a beautiful silver censer.

Next day, our travellers continued their route

toward Mount Gargano. Gerard, although exhausted with fatigue, wished to make the ascent on foot in honor of the Archangel. Having reached the holy grotto, the young pilgrims prayed long and earnestly. But when it was time to withdraw, they found Brother Gerard in ecstasy. On returning to consciousness, he said, "It is nothing. Let us get something to eat," and descending to the inn, he called for supper.

The next morning was also consecrated to the glorious Archangel. Dinner hour having come, Gerard told his young companions to sit down at table. At this order, they regarded him with astonishment, for they thought the purse empty. "Men of little faith," said Gerard to them, "sit down at table!" Then giving some money to the hermit, he requested him to go buy some bread. The latter went downstairs and returned quickly. But what did he see? A table covered with fish and Gerard distributing to everyone his share. Could God, who takes care of the little birds, forget His children? A witness relates that the good brother, seeing the purse empty, went to commend himself to the holy Archangel. Soon, someone came to him and put in his hand a roll of money.

When they were leaving Mount Gargano, the innkeeper exacted an exorbitant price. Gerard, indignant at the injustice, said to him, "If you are not satisfied with what is due you, you will be punished. Your mules will die." Hardly had he uttered these words when the innkeeper's son ran up to his father in great distress, crying: "Come quickly! Come quickly! I do not know what is the matter with the mules. They are rolling on the ground in a dreadful way. Quick! Quick!" The innkeeper, turning pale, cast himself in fright at Gerard's feet. "I forgive you," said the Saint, "but never forget that God is with His poor. Woe to you if you ever again ask more than is due you!" Then he went to the mules, made the Sign of the Cross over them and cured them instantly. He paid the innkeeper and departed.

Water is sometimes very scarce in these parts of Italy. There lived at the foot of Mount Gargano a proprietor who carried his hard-heartedness so far as to refuse water from his wells to thirsty pilgrims. Our young travellers having asked for some, he refused them point-blank. After some useless entreaties, Gerard said to him sternly: "You refuse water to your neighbor whom you ought to love as yourself. Now see, the well in its turn will refuse it to you." With these words, he turned away, and immediately the well dried up.

Seeing this, the proprietor ran in all haste after Gerard, begging him to have pity on him. "Ah, come back!" he cried in a pitiful voice. "Come back, and you shall have drink, all of you and all your beasts!"

"In charity, my brother," replied Gerard, "never refuse to anyone the water that belongs to everyone; otherwise, God will refuse it to you." The man promised earnestly. Then, at the order of the Saint, water again filled the well, and his companions were able to slake their thirst at their pleasure.

These were not the only marvels of that homeward journey. The little caravan was hungry, and there was no food. Gerard, always confiding in Providence, began to make a bouquet of flowers. When it was finished, he went and placed it before the holy Tabernacle of a church. He said to Jesus Christ: "Lord, my little family has nothing to eat." Soon two servants appeared, each with a basket of provisions for the hungry travellers. After renewing their strength, they reached the city of Foggia, where another benefactor offered them hospitality.

Next day, they went to visit the celebrated sanctuary of the Virgin Crowned, about two thirds of a mile from Foggia. Hardly had Gerard seen the image of her whom he called "his only joy," than he was rapt in ecstasy. When he recovered his senses, they asked him what was the matter. "Nothing," he answered. "It is a weakness to which I am subject."

When passing through Troia, they went to venerate a miraculous picture of Christ, the sight of which was so touching that one could not look at it without emotion. Gerard, the lover of the Crucified, on beholding it, experienced transports of love visible to all.

And so this pilgrimage was but a long chain of prodigies. It lasted nine days, and our pilgrims returned to the convent with the purse better supplied than when they set out.

7. CHARITY TO HIS NEIGHBOR

THE love of God and of one's neighbor are insep-
arable. They are two rivulets flowing from the
same source. The Apostle St. John hesitated not to
say: "If any man say, I love God, and hateth his
brother, he is a liar." (*1 John* 4:20). Gerard perfectly
fulfilled the precept of charity. Jesus Christ present
in the Eucharist and Jesus Christ present in the sick
and the poor—such were the two great attractions
of his heart. "The infirm and the needy," he used to
say, "are Christ visible; the Blessed Sacrament is
Christ invisible."

This supernatural charity made him, above all,
entirely devoted to this confreres. "When I see a
Father or a brother in need," he used to say, "I will
quit everything else to help him." During a rigorous winter, he gave up his waistcoat to a confrere
and kept only a light soutane (cassock) for himself.
To yield to others all that was most comfortable was
one of his favorite maxims. He had made the resolution to visit his sick brethren several times a day
and to render them all the services imaginable.

As soon as he arrived at Caposele, he began to
serve Brother Pietro Picone, a young student who
was dying of consumption (tuberculosis). Gerard succeeded so well in gaining his good graces that the
invalid knew not how to do without him. One night
among others, he begged Brother Nicolo, who was
sitting up with him, to go bring Brother Gerard to
help him. Brother Nicolo thought it well to refuse,

since it was midnight. But what was his astonishment to behold Brother Gerard appear and offer his services to the dear invalid, who had the consolation of dying some days later in the arms of the Saint!

His tender and compassionate soul led Gerard to desire to take upon himself the sufferings and pains of his brethren. During his stay at Naples, Father Margotta passed through the crucible of the most painful interior desolation.

One day, when more than ordinarily afflicted, he said to Brother Gerard: "Let us go to the church of St. George and pray to Our Lady of Help."

"Yes, let us go," replied the brother, "but you will not obtain the favor you desire." In truth, the Father returned home more troubled than when he went.

About this time, Gerard was transferred from Naples to Caposele. He was writing a letter one day when Doctor Santorelli entered his room. The good brother said to him: "I am writing to Father Margotta to tell him that he is freed from his trial, and to congratulate him." That same day, the sufferings of the good priest came to an end, but—oh, miracle of charity—Gerard himself on that day became pale, sad and dejected! The Father Rector inquired the reason for the change in his appearance. "Not having the courage to see Father Margotta suffering any longer," was the reply, "I offered myself to Jesus Christ to suffer in his stead."

His compassionate charity showed itself as well toward strangers as toward his brethren. He loved to say: "I would give my life a thousand times, if that were possible, to render service to my neighbor." A Canon of Melfi fell seriously ill in our convent of Iliceto. Gerard lavished on him the most assiduous care, leaving him neither day nor night. The sick man had no idea that he was receiving this last attention. But having awakened one night, what was his surprise to find Gerard by his side, full of solicitude for him! This admirable charity made so deep an impression on him that he ever after published the sanctity of the servant of God.

Gerard often visited the Hospital of the Incurables at Naples. A mother was never more tender to her child than he was toward the suffering members of Jesus Christ. It was an admirable sight to behold him going from bed to bed, encouraging some to patience, preparing others for death, lavishing on all whatever relief lay in his power.

Even the insane were the objects of his charity. He consoled these unfortunates with so much kindness that, as soon as they saw him enter, they ran to meet him full of joy. "Dear Father," they would say, "you are so good! Stay with us all the time. Do not leave us. No, no, we do not want you to go! No one says such beautiful things to us as you do. Your lips are lips of Paradise, and we want to listen to you all the time."

How often he aided his neighbor at the risk of his own life! Going one day from Melfi to Atella with some candidates for ordination, he met several men who could not go to their work on account of the rising of a river. What did Gerard do? Crossing the torrent on horseback, he took them all over behind him, one after another. To some who cried out to him not to expose himself so, he replied: "The love of our neighbor!" To encourage his beast, he would say: "Let us go on, good horse! We are pleasing our God." On reaching another river swollen like the first, he passed the young clerics over in the same way, going and returning for each one until all were safe on the other side.

One day he met an old man of Iliceto carrying on his head a heavy load of wood. The charitable brother took his burden and would not lay it down until he reached the poor man's hut. He rendered a similar service to an old woman who was climbing up the heights of St. Agatha with a heavy basket of wet linen on her head. In spite of the repugnance that he felt to entering the city in such a manner, Gerard put down the basket only before the poor woman's house.

The misery of the poor pierced his heart. Many a time he was seen taking off his shoes to give them to some beggar. It is without doubt due to his tender commiseration for the miseries of humanity that we must attribute the gift of miracles so largely bestowed by the Divine Master on His faithful servant. To see misery and not to relieve it would have been something very painful to the heart of Gerard, and the kind Heart of Jesus had to provide for that.

When he was stationed at the convent of Caposele, the charge of porter was confided to him. Happy in being chosen for that employment, he exclaimed: "This key will be for me the key of Paradise!" This duty was especially dear to him because it entailed the care of the poor, whom he venerated as his superiors and the dear friends of Christ. Although a multitude presented themselves daily, Gerard possessed the very difficult art of satisfying everyone. Their tricks, their impertinence, could never weary his patience. He knew very well that they were deceiving him sometimes by presenting themselves more than once, but he feigned not to perceive it. Knowing the miseries of the unfortunate, he would say: "These are the robbers who render us dear to Jesus Christ."

Above all was his charity to be admired toward those whom sickness prevented from coming to the door. When they sent their children or some relative to receive alms for them, he always took care to satisfy them. He was willing to fast himself that he might be able to relieve them, and God was pleased to show by miracles how agreeable to Him was his charity.

One morning, as fast as the poor arrived, Gerard ran to the kitchen to get them their share. The cook, seeing that there was no end to it, said to him: "What are you about? What will be left for the Community?"

"God will provide," answered the good brother.

The cook, not at all appeased, muttered: "We'll see how it will end."

The dinner hour having arrived, he found to his great astonishment that the quantity of food, very far from diminishing, was increased, for, after the whole Community had been abundantly supplied, there remained sufficient to satisfy many others who again presented themselves.

When Gerard could not get food suitable for the sick from the kitchen, he sent them some white bread with a little cheese, that they might be able to recover their strength. He used to search the pantry, and when he found some sweetmeats, he would joyfully send them, saying with the most loving accent: "We ought to sacrifice everything for the poor, for they are the living image of Jesus Christ." Gerard had at Caposele a means of satisfying his charity that he had not at Iliceto. The convent had a central location, so he could more easily visit the sick when he went out on errands. His mere presence sufficed to console them and lead them to resignation to the will of God.

The charity of the holy religious was not limited to relieving the ordinary indigent. How many shame-faced poor, how many widows, orphans, married people, men out of work, turned to him for assistance in their miseries! How many young persons did he help, some to a respectable marriage, others to enter the convent! Providence never failed to second him in his pious and charitable desires.

8. HIS CHARITY IN TIME OF DREADFUL DISTRESS

GERARD'S charity to the poor was remarkable during the winter of 1754-1755. The frost, snow and excessive cold prevented laborers from earning their bread, and famine was severely felt in the mountainous districts of Caposele. Every morning, over two hundred famished creatures presented themselves at the convent gate—men, women and old people. The rector, Father Cajone, touched at their extreme misery, sent for Brother Gerard one day and said to him: "I order you to provide for the necessities of these unfortunate creatures. Their fate is in your hands. If you do not help them, they must die. I give you full authority over all in the house. Dispose of it as you wish." These words filled Gerard with joy, and he neglected nothing by which he might succor the needy.

He found it a favorable time to distribute spiritual as well as corporal alms. He gave his dear protegees familiar instructions, always illustrating his teaching by edifying examples. When it became known that he was holding catechetical instructions, many persons in easy circumstances desired to assist at them, and even noble ladies were seen mingling with the poor to hear him speak of the things of God. The chief care of the charitable brother was to prepare souls for a good Confession. He ceased not to beg Our Lord to touch hardened hearts and to spare them the chastisements of His just vengeance. His zeal and prayers were so pleasing to Almighty God that it was a daily occurrence to see, leaving his instruction, souls touched by grace, hurrying to cast themselves at the feet of a confessor.

Among the conversions of which he was the

instrument is related that of a young girl who had lived long in the habit of sin and sacrilege. She had had the skill even to deceive certain confessors, who looked upon her as a Saint. Gerard, perceiving her one day better disposed than usual in consequence of his instructions, showed her the danger of her state. He then sent her to Father Fiocchi, to whom she confessed with torrents of tears. Thenceforth she was for the whole city of Caposele a true model of piety, modesty and penitence.

The cold and its consequent famine became daily more rigorous. Gerard was so touched with pity for the good workmen who came to him every day as to their father that he kept several large fires burning in the vestibule of the house to warm them. He showed special tenderness for the little children, and pointing them out to their elders, he would say, "It is we who have sinned, and these dear innocents have to bear the penalty." Then he would melt into tears. Taking the hands of the poor little ones, he would warm them in his own, beholding in them the image of Jesus Christ suffering for the sins of men.

The holy brother also took upon himself the duty of clothing these poor unfortunates, who were shivering with cold. Strong in the permission he had received, he visited the wardrobe and despoiled it of everything he thought would suit his purpose. During this rigorous season, he gave to the beloved poor of the good God his own waistcoat and cloak.

Not satisfied with clothing and warming the members of Jesus Christ, the Saint also had to feed them, and he did it with the generosity of a man who doubts not the treasures of Divine Providence. Many a time did Our Lord make known how pleasing to Him was this confidence. Without a miracle, in fact, it would have been impossible for Gerard to discharge the ministry that obedience had imposed on him. "Three or four times," related Father Cajone on this subject, "the good brother came to bring me a considerable sum of money, which he said he had found in the box at the gate. From whence did this money come? That is the secret of God and the good brother. As for myself, I know nothing about it."

Food visibly multiplied in his hands. The baker saw one evening that Gerard had distributed all the bread, and there remained but a very slim supply for the Community. He went to complain to the Rector. Father Cajone sent for the culprit and reproved him for his indiscreet bounty, since the late hour prevented the purchase of more bread in the city. "Fear nothing, dear Father," replied the friend of the poor, "the good God will take care of us." Then turning to the baker, he said to him: "Dear Brother, let us go see. There may be some left." The baker, declaring there was none, opened the bread-press. It was full! "Oh," cried Gerard, "may God be forever blessed!" And he ran off to the church to thank Him. The other brother, truly amazed, said to Father Cajone, who now appeared, "O dear Father, Gerard is a real Saint! I assure you there was not left a single loaf, and now we have a number of loaves. It is God who has done it!"

"Yes," replied the Rector, "It is God. Truly, the Lord plays with Gerard."

This occurrence was frequently repeated. A student assisted one day at the distribution of bread. He affirmed that the baskets, as soon as emptied, were at once refilled without visible help. Another related that, having distributed with his own hands all the bread contained in a large box, without much thought he happened to open it again—and found it refilled. Certainly, had not God provided in this way, the supplies of the house would have been wholly insufficient for the support of so many poor families during a famine of several months.

It was a happy thing that Gerard, the "Father of the Poor," as they called him, was on the spot. Dr. Santorelli warned him one day to use a certain measure of discretion in his almsgiving, not to give bread to all indiscriminately, but only to the really needy. "We must give to all," replied Gerard, "since all ask it for the love of Jesus Christ; otherwise, Jesus Christ would no longer multiply the loaves."

The provisions of the granary were, however, almost exhausted. The Father Rector, thinking they ought not to tempt Almighty God, felt it his duty to moderate the generosity of the charitable brother.

"Have no anxiety, dear Father," said Gerard. "God will provide."

"You want miracles, whether or not," replied the Superior, and he went to inspect the granary. Oh, bounty of Divine Providence! It was over-flowing with the finest wheat.

On a certain feast day, Gerard conceived the idea of having a grand entertainment for his poor friends. He begged some of the other brothers to help him, got a large quantity of flour and began to prepare macaroni. After cooking a goodly portion of it, full of joy, he began to distribute it among his numerous guests. But so great was their number that the quantity prepared was quite insufficient. Not at all disconcerted, the Saint went on confidently handing it around. Very far from running short, there was an abundance for all and much left over.

Here is something still more marvelous. A woman of the higher classes, constrained by hunger, entered the vestibule one morning with the poor, but she stood apart, deterred by shame from presenting herself with the rest. Gerard, having finished his distribution and not suspecting that this person was in need, was about to withdraw. It was in truth no rare thing for persons of good condition to assist through devotion at the instructions of the saintly brother, to witness the beautiful spectacle of his charity. Someone called his attention to the lady, but his store was gone. "O God!" exclaimed Gerard with emotion, "why did You not say something to me?" He reflected an instant, hurried into the house and, returning immediately, took from a fold of his garment a little loaf still warm, as if just from the oven. Now at that very moment, the oven was cold, and the loaf was in shape very unlike the loaves used in the community.

Two daughters of a good workman also received

under similar circumstances two little miraculous
loaves. So great was the faith of the people in these
marvels that well-to-do persons of Caposele used to
send their children to mingle with the poor, in order
to receive a *little white loaf from Paradise.*

9. HIS CHARITY TOWARD HIS ENEMIES

THE perfection of charity is the love of enemies
and doing good to them. This was Gerard's
way of acting.

The road leading from Iliceto to Foggia passed
through the center of the grounds belonging to the
Duke of Bovino. The nobleman, unwilling to have
his domain so cut up, ordered his overseers to hinder the right of passage. One day, Gerard was
returning from Foggia. Not knowing the recent prohibition, he followed the old road as hitherto. The
man in charge at the time was a monster of cruelty.
As soon as he saw the humble brother, he fell upon
him and loaded him with blows so violent with the
butt-end of his gun that the poor religious fell from
his horse all battered and bruised. Even then, the
savage continued to maltreat him, driving his gun
into his back and his breast. "For a long time," he
cried, "I have been watching for a monk on whom
to glut my hatred. Oh, you have come just in time!"
Gerard struggled to his knees as best he could and
begged for mercy, alleging his ignorance of the prohibition. "No excuses!" cried the man, still more
infuriated, and he went on striking without pity.

"Strike, dear brother," said Gerard, "strike, for you are right!" And he ceased not to repeat with joined hands: "Strike, for you are right!"

The guard, confused at such patience, entered into himself and cried out: "Oh, what have I done? I have killed a Saint!" In his turn he cast himself at Gerard's feet to ask pardon. The latter embraced him, renewed his excuses for his involuntary trespass and then, feeling unable to mount his horse, begged his aggressor to help him into the saddle and support him to the convent.

On the way, instead of complaining, he tried to convert him, representing to him what an evil thing it is to offend God and to deserve Hell. On arriving half-dead at the convent, the saintly Redemptorist said that he had fallen from his horse, but not a word of the cruel treatment he had received. On the contrary, here shone his virtue. He had the man well treated "for the charity," he said, "that he had shown him."

The justice of God, however, was not slow in punishing the guilty one. Not long after, he was shot under similar circumstances. On learning this, Gerard wept as if for the death of an intimate friend, although the blows he had received from the man so affected his chest that ever after he was subject to spitting blood. As hard on himself as he was tender to others, he paid no attention to his own ills and never even spoke of them. A brother surprised him one day in the midst of a hemorrhage. As he wanted to apprise the Superior at once, Brother

Gerard said with ineffable humility: "O dear Brother, say nothing about it, I beg you. This happens to me frequently, and I do not think it my duty to speak to anyone about it."

10. HIS PROFOUND HUMILITY

TRUE virtue can rest only on the foundation of profound humility. The life of Gerard proves this. His confreres vied with one another in calling him the ideal of humility. "Gerard," says one of them, "esteemed himself the last and the worst of the brothers. He called himself a miserable creature, a sinner, a worthless nothing." Filled with horror of self, he considered himself a monster whom the earth ought to engulf. He eagerly sought and discharged with joy the most menial employments, such as the care of animals, renewing their litter and clearing away the manure. Meeting one day the Bishop of Melfi, who was very desirous of seeing him, he said to him: "Alas! Who am I that Monsignor wants to speak to me? I am only a worm of the earth, a sinner, a miserable creature, who has need of all the mercy of God."

Among all his miracles, the greatest was his humility in the midst of honors. Few Saints were favored with gifts so extraordinary, and yet he never took the least vanity in them. This was what most impressed those who had the happiness of dealing with him. He had a horror of praise, and the mere shadow of esteem forced him to run and hide himself. He would have wished to lead a life entirely hidden.

One day, coming to a place where he was unknown, he fell on his knees and, thinking himself alone, exclaimed: "Lord, I thank Thee, for no one knows me here!"

The noblemen De Philippi of Serino, having heard of the miracles he everywhere performed, conceived a great desire to see him. The Saint, who knew it, was one day passing by Serino, and he went to the inn. As soon as these gentlemen—who were very devoted to the sons of St. Alphonsus—heard that a Redemptorist was in their neighborhood, they sent for him. Gerard went then to the chateau, but knew so well how to disguise himself that they never suspected that he was the brother of whom they had heard such great things.

In his humility, he envied the little and the lowly, whom the contempt of this world rendered more like unto Jesus Christ. Seeing one day a poor messenger soaked with rain and covered with mud, he exclaimed: "I would purchase at any price the condition of this poor man, who for a morsel of bread has to expose himself to the rebuffs and contempt of everyone, while I . . ." and without finishing, he burst into tears.

Humiliations and contempt are the touchstone of humility. One day, when Gerard was at Naples, a beggar insulted him grossly. Someone wanted to punish the latter, but Gerard interceded for him. "Oh, that is nothing!" he said. "I am a sinner, a miserable creature. He wanted only to joke a little."

A Canon of Conza, named Camillus Bozzio, one day tested the virtue of the saintly brother. He was preaching the Lent at Atella when Gerard arrived there. Seeing the latter in the sacristy in the midst of priests and laymen, who were listening to him as to an oracle, he said to him brusquely and contemptuously: "What are you saying there? You are only an ignorant brother, and you wish to play the theologian. . . .I look upon you as a vain and hypocritical man." These words, so humiliating, far from disturbing the brother's serenity, filled him with joy. Both the Canon and Gerard were staying at the time with the Grazioli family. Now, that same day, the former by chance entered the room of the servant of God and found him raised in the air in ecstasy.

One day, Father Fiocchi was conversing in the parlor with the Carmelites of Ripacandida. Suddenly he turned toward Gerard, who was with him, and in a rough tone ordered him to leave the room. Then the Father expressed to the religious his profound veneration for the friend whom he had just humbled. "Oh, how like this brother is to the Divine Master!" he said. "He really has the face of Jesus Crucified."

Gerard's humility shone not less at Naples in the midst of the concourse of people that gathered around him.

One day, when he was alone in the house, a liveried servant presented himself, begging that Brother Gerard should be sent to the home of the Duchess of Maddaloni. Seeing that the messenger did not know him, Gerard replied: "I cannot understand how anyone can want that brother. He is only a simpleton, a half-fool. They are strangely deceived in his regard here in Naples. Tell the Duchess that." The noble lady understood very well that such an answer could come from none but Gerard himself. Next day, she went to the church where the Saint was accustomed to hear Mass. As soon as she saw him, she implored him to cure her child, who was ill. "Behold," said Gerard to her, pointing to the Blessed Sacrament, "behold Him who dispenses graces," and he promised to pray for the child. The Duchess had not yet left the church when a messenger came to tell her that the child was cured.

As a preservative against vainglory, the humble son of St. Alphonsus loved to mingle with the poor and beg with them a morsel of bread. More than once he was seen holding out his hand at the gate of the Seminary of Muro, his own city, and among the religious of the Oratory at Naples. It was only through obedience that he gave up this practice.

11. HIS MORTIFICATION

HUMILITY gives birth to renunciation of self and so Gerard became his own executioner. He was a lifelong enemy to indulgence of the appetite. He took scarcely two ounces of bread a day, and when they constrained him to eat some meat, he was careful to season it with bitter powders. "The love of God," he used to say, "does not enter into the soul if the body is too well fed." During meals, he appeared wholly absorbed in God. He was often seen out of himself, bread in one hand, a fork in the other, with his eyes bathed in tears and as if ravished in ecstasy.

When at Melfi with Father Stefano di Liguori, he could not prevent their seeing him put bitter powder on what had been served him. His companion tried some macaroni thus seasoned, but he found it so bitter that he was forced to reject it. This passionate lover of the Cross once confessed to Dr. Santorelli that for three whole years he had begged Our Lord to deprive him of the sense of taste and that at last he had been heard, "so that a pumpkin now has as much relish for me as a chicken," he said.

"Ask for nothing." This was the maxim of him whom they called "a prodigy of mortification." When he returned home, worn out with fatigue and bathed in perspiration, he asked for nothing. This perfect self-renunciation was worth as much to him as mortifications. He was sent one day to Accadia, just under 10 miles from Iliceto. He started at once without breaking his fast, but on his arrival, he fell unconscious.

His mortification conducted him to the perfection of evangelical poverty. He longed to be the most indifferently fed, clothed and lodged of all his brethren. The remains of the table were his food by preference. He sought out the habits most worn, though he esteemed it a virtue to be always very clean.

At Iliceto, he chose for his cell an alcove into which a ray of light never penetrated. His bed, or to speak more truly, his instrument of torture, was a straw mattress, which the narrow alcove could scarcely accommodate, and a couple of tiles were his pillow. One day, a brother had the curiosity to examine this couch. He found it filled with stones and thorns and surrounded with human skulls (a reminder of death).

When an ordinary cell was assigned him, he hardly ever used it, for he resigned it to any visitor who happened to come. On such occasions, he took his rest on the floor or on some straw out in the stable.

Frequently at Iliceto he spent the night under the main altar, which was hollow. In this nook so delightful to his piety, he once had a somewhat amusing adventure. After very probably having passed the greater part of the night in prayer, he slept so soundly toward morning that he awoke only at the Sanctus of the first Mass. This was followed by a second and a third Mass, so that Gerard, in order not to betray his mortification and astonish the faithful, had to remain in his hiding place until all the Masses were over.

He was commanded later on to make use of an ordinary mattress, but by his entreaties he obtained from his director permission to sleep three nights in the week on a plank with two tiles for a pillow, a large stone hung on his feet and his person covered by an instrument of penance. When absent from the convent, he slept on the bare floor, but to conceal his penance, he took care to leave the bed-clothes in disorder.

The instruments he used to crucify his flesh were of such a nature that they made the beholder shudder. He scourged himself once or twice daily with a discipline of wet cords. On Fridays and the eves of feasts, he scourged himself to blood with a steel discipline armed with twelve sharp-pointed stars. His body was never without wounds. He wore almost constantly around his person an iron chain armed with points. Similar chains encircled his arms and lower limbs. He knew not what punishment to invent for self-torture. It was almost a miracle that he could discharge his duties while practicing these terrible austerities.

Jesus Crucified was his great book, and the more he read in it, the less pity he had for himself. We have seen to what excess he carried the holy folly of the Cross. The love of Jesus Crucified made him so passionately desirous of sufferings that he would willingly have daily reproduced in his own person the dolorous scenes of the Passion. No doubt, after his profession he frequently solicited permission to renew the barbarous tortures to which he had subjected himself during his youth at Muro, and at Iliceto during his first and second novitiates, but it does not appear that the permission was granted.

12. HIS ANGELIC PURITY

GERARD'S excessive mortifications had the happy effect of preserving the precious lily of chastity unstained. Only an Angel from Heaven could make known the purity of this holy religious. All his directors have attested that he was one of the purest, most beautiful, most innocent, most privileged souls that could be found on earth. All who had the happiness of living in intimate communion with him called him "an earthly Angel, a model of innocence, a marvel of penance, the ideal of every virtue." His beautiful soul is reflected in these words, which we have already given among his resolutions: "Of all the virtues dear to me, O my God, that which I love with predilection is purity and divine candor. I firmly hope from Thee, O infinite Purity, the grace to be preserved from every thought that might sully my soul!"

To preserve this inestimable treasure, the angelic Gerard knew how to unite the simplicity of the dove with all the prudence of the serpent. It was owing to this that he made it a rule never to converse alone with a person of the other sex. We read in his resolutions the following practice: "I will say an *Ave Maria* in honor of the purity of the Blessed Virgin every time a woman presents herself before me." He watched with most scrupulous attention over his heart. "An affection which draws us ever so little from God," he used to say, "is a firebrand of Hell. Our affections ought to be most pure. We should love all things in God." He practiced detachment of heart even toward his family, to whom on parting he left this testament: "I go away to become a Saint. Forget me."

What delighted the religious sisters with whom he had communion, either by word or letter, was his extreme modesty and the profound respect he evinced toward them, beholding in them the spouses of Jesus Christ and the images of the Blessed Virgin. "The only reason for my writing to you," he said in one of his letters, "is that all of you, spouses of my Divine Master, represent to me the Divine Mother."

It seems as if God willed to reward in diverse ways this admirable purity of the angelic Redemptorist: first, by dispensing to him with extraordinary prodigality those supernatural gifts that recall the original innocence of the first man; secondly, by according him the privilege of making virginity loved to such a degree that he had the happiness of offering to God a host of virgins; and lastly, by endowing his cincture with the special power of curing sickness and putting the demons to flight.

God several times showed by exemplary chastisements the care that he took of the exquisite purity of His servant. When in Naples, Gerard frequented the church of Spirito Santo. Two women of bad reputation never failed, as he passed, to insult his humility and modesty, and once they had the effrontery to bar his passage. At this Gerard paused, indignant: "You will not desist? Would you experience the justice of God?" Hardly had he uttered the words when one of them fell as if struck by lightning and died exclaiming: "O Madonna, I am dying! O Madonna, I am dying!"

We shall see later on how a black calumny launched against the reputation of the virginal religious served only to give to his virtue still greater luster.

13. HIS SPIRIT OF PRAYER

GERARD knew perfectly how to unite the duties of Martha and Mary, to unite labor and prayer, the active with the contemplative life. Grace had given him such liberty of spirit that the most numerous, most fatiguing occupations never interrupted his union with God. He prayed always, and with faith so lively that one would have said he saw the Lord. Prayer was his attraction, his life, his nourishment, his delight. It was his center, outside of which he could find no rest.

"Labor," says Father Tannoia, his biographer, "was for Gerard no obstacle to the spirit of prayer, for though he worked much by day, by night he withdrew into the church, where he melted into tears before the Blessed Sacrament. As the exercises of piety prescribed by the Rule were insufficient to satisfy his heart, he indemnified himself by night, so that when morning dawned, he was found still at the place he had taken the preceding evening. Everything was a prayer for him. Whatever might be his occupation, he never forgot the presence of God.

Everywhere and always his recollection of spirit was profound, his ejaculatory prayers frequent and fervent. Jesus and Mary were constantly in his heart and on his lips. Sometimes he was so absorbed in God that he was seen to stop short in the midst of his work."

His recollection was more of Heaven than of earth. After his death, one of his confessors, Father de Robertis, did not hesitate to affirm that this admirable religious passed not one moment, so to speak, without actually thinking of God. One day at the Chapter of Faults he received an obedience not to think of God. But what could he do against Him who attracted him so irresistibly? Not to fail in obedience, a struggle then began between him and the Object of his love. "O my God," he was heard to sigh in the corridors of the house, "O my God, I do not want to think of Thee, I do not want to think of Thee!"

When journeying, he was at times so lost in God that he forgot his way. One day, he was much astonished to find himself at Foggia instead of at Melfi, where he should have been. Father Juvenal could not sufficiently admire the angelic recollection of the servant of God. "When he gave me an account of his interior life," said this able director, "Gerard confessed to me that he could not help thinking of God and that he had to do unheard-of violence to himself to turn away from the thought."

Whatever helped him to think of his Well-Beloved was dear to him. "Dear Brother," said Dr. Santorelli to him one day in summer, "oh, how this intense heat multiplies the mosquitoes! How do you pass the night in their company?"

"Oh, I am under great obligation to them!" answered Gerard. "They keep me from sleeping, and so I can think of God the whole night long."

All who gave him hospitality thought naturally of the Seraphim always in contemplation before the throne of the Most High. Never did he emerge from his deep recollection. He either spoke of God or he spoke to God. He perfumed the earth with his virtue and piety because his conversation was in Heaven.

One evening he was at the house of Don Salvadore at Oliveto when he began to speak of the divine perfections with such knowledge, love and fervor that he seemed to be one of the Blessed descended from Heaven and entirely transformed into God. The archpriest, who was drinking in the words of this seraphic soul, at last noticed the advanced hour of the night and apprised his guest of it. The latter responded by a deep sigh, and when asked the reason, he said: "O God! how miserable we are, since all the time that we give to sleep might be employed in thinking of God, our well-beloved Lord."

We may say that Gerard had no other guide in the ways of prayer than the Holy Spirit Himself, with whom from his infancy he had contracted a holy alliance. "I choose the Holy Spirit," we read in his resolutions, "for my only Consoler and Protector in all things. May He be my justification, and may He root out all my faults!" "He passed not a day," one of his confidants tells us—"what do I say?—he let no hour go by without invoking Him. He did so above all when asked for advice or when he himself had need of light. The mere thought of the Holy Spirit ravished his soul and transfigured his countenance. But above all, on the day of Pentecost he was seen transported with joy. Every year, to prepare better for the solemnity, he redoubled his fasts and penances, and whoever met him on that day, however tepid before, experienced some of the fiery ardor that inflamed his soul."

From hence arose the attraction for the life of prayer which he knew how to breathe into fervent souls. Many priests, distinguished for their exemplary life and zeal for the salvation of souls, drew from the counsel of our celestial Redemptorist that spirit of prayer which gives to the apostolate its fruitfulness and to Christian works the divine sanctifying sap.

All nature was for this pure soul a poem in which everything sang of the glory and love of the Creator. The stars, the hills, the flowers, the fruits, the birds, the animals—all spoke to him of God, all ravished him in God. One day he saw at a distance in one of the streets of Caposele a cock. The sight of the fowl with its rich plumage elevated his thoughts, dilated his heart. "Come here, creature of my God!" he cried. And instantly, as if it understood the words addressed to it, the cock ran to his feet, flapping its wings and making the air resound with its crowing. Gerard tenderly caressed it and for half an hour was transported out of himself.

The arts, whose true end is to elevate the heart to God, produced on the noble and sensitive soul of Gerard all their sublime effects. How often, at the sight of a statue of Christ carved by an able hand, or of a picture of the Blessed Virgin artistically painted, was he seen to fall into ecstasy! How often did music and singing elevate him to the concert of the Angels!

Among the boarding students of the Sisters of Saint Saviour at Foggia there was one child gifted with the voice of an Angel. One day she was present at a conference that Gerard gave the nuns in the parlor. At the request of the brother, the child began to sing a canticle on divine love. Immediately the servant of God became radiant as a Seraph, and, his hands crossed on his breast, eyes raised to Heaven, he fell into ecstasy.

14. HIS OBEDIENCE

ALL saintly religious have excelled in obedience, but I know not whether there was one who carried the simplicity and heroism of this virtue so far as our good Brother Gerard. He is called—and justly so—the "Saint of Obedience." As with holy folly he sought to reproduce in himself the Passion of Our Lord, so did he will by that same holy folly to become a perfect copy of Him who was obedient unto death, even the death of the Cross. Terrestrial Seraph, he had the same desire as the celestial Seraphim, to do always and in everything the will of God, to consume himself with love for the amiable Divine Will. "O Will of God!" he loved to repeat, his eyes fixed on Heaven and with an accent of inimitable love, "O Will of God!" He experienced the need of obeying as the heavenly spirits experience the necessity of loving God and of proving to Him their love by the promptitude of their submission.

His obedience was altogether supernatural: "My Jesus," he would say, "for love of Thee I will obey my Superiors as Thy Divine Person rendered visible." And in fact, if Jesus Christ in person had given him his orders, Gerard could not have obeyed more promptly nor more perfectly. He adored the will of his Superiors. "The will of my Divine Master," he would say, "is identified with that of my Superiors." From hence came his resolution: "These words: *I will* and *I will not,* shall be strangers to me. I will but one thing: Thy Will, O my God, and not mine!"

He desired to practice not a mutilated obedience, but an obedience whole, entire, universal. "Why lose, even in the smallest actions, the merit of obedience?" he would say. He observed the least rules as scrupulously as if there were question of avoiding a grave fault. "He who fails in little things," he loved to say, "exposes himself thereby to fail in great, for God punishes little multiplied faults by permitting grave ones." It was to shun this misfortune that he composed the prayer: "Give me, O Lord, the courage to observe Thy law faithfully. Alas! If I had the misfortune to wander a little, it would not be long before I should wander a great deal, for Thou dost permit him who from levity of heart allows himself small infractions to end by being drawn into frightful errors."

Embodying the ideal of a Redemptorist Brother, such as St. Alphonsus desired him to be, the Saint wished to know no other code of perfection than his Rules. He knew them by heart, so assiduously had he read them and meditated on them. His confreres used to say: "If the Constitutions of the Institute happened to be lost, Brother Gerard could write them again without omitting a comma."

He obeyed with the simplicity of a child. Once Father Cafaro enjoined upon him to render an account of his interior to a lay brother. He did it without delay and with the same exactitude as to his director.

He had so much confidence in obedience that with it he feared no danger. One day when he was at Carbonara, Father Fiocchi called him to Melfi. A deluge of rain was falling at the time. His host, Don Antonio de Dominico, seeing that he could not set out in such weather without running the risk of his life—on account of the torrents he would have to cross—tried to detain him. But the obedient Redemptorist would go at any cost. "Obedience wills it," he said. And when it was objected that obedience might be interpreted, Gerard replied: "For the love of Our Lord, insist no longer. I declare to you that the storm will abate as soon as I leave the house." Wondering at such virtue, his host exclaimed: "What admirable obedience!"

As he had predicted, as soon as he began the journey, the rain ceased. Two men accompanied him to the dreaded torrent of Ofanto. The river was rolling in waves so furious that they uprooted and carried away trees a hundred years old. Not at all daunted, the servant of God said to his horse: "Let us go over in the name of the Most Holy Trinity." He had reached the middle of the river when a huge tree came rapidly down the stream, borne along by the swift current. Without a miracle, it would have been all over with Gerard. But he, making the Sign of the Cross on the tree, arrested its course and passed on safe and sound. On arriving at Lacedonia, he related the fact to Msgr. Amato, saying: "See what obedience can do!"

Every word of superiors was sacred for this good religious, and we may say that he sometimes carried the simplicity of obedience to a degree that seemed more worthy of admiration than of imitation. Our Lord was pleased to favor his obedience by giving him an intuitive knowledge of the wishes of superiors. The latter, aware of this particular gift of Gerard, failed not when occasion offered to make use of it. They were sure that, far or near, their orders would be fulfilled.

One day, Father Fiocchi being at Melfi, at the house of Msgr. Basta, their conversation turned to Gerard's holy life. The Bishop had long desired to see him, and he begged to be allowed to send for him. "It is not necessary, Monsignor, to send for him," replied Father Fiocchi. "It is sufficient for me to command him, even at a distance, to come to Melfi, and he will present himself immediately. You can then see how far his obedience extends."

Thereupon the priest recollected himself and mentally ordered Gerard to come to him. On his arrival, the Rector feigned to receive him coldly. "What brought you here?" he asked.

"The obedience you gave me," answered the brother modestly.

"What! I did not order you here, neither by letter nor by dispatch."

"No," replied Gerard, "but you gave me a formal order to come to you. Monsignor wants to see me."

This miraculous obedience filled the Bishop with the most profound veneration for the Saint, and he wanted to keep him with him for almost a month. One day, when at Corato, Gerard suddenly told his hosts of his resolution to start for Iliceto, but they begged him to defer his departure. "I must return," he replied, "my superior is calling me." They learned later that Father Fiocchi had mentally given him an order to go home.

When the will of superiors was signified to him, Gerard doubted not of its accomplishment, even if a miracle were necessary. One day he met a wealthy lady in Caposele, from whom he begged for a little white silk to make a veil for the holy ciborium. Not being able to find any to suit, the lady conceived the idea of cutting a piece from her wedding dress. Gerard, to whom her thought was revealed, seeing her the next day, told her not to spoil the gown.

"Look again," said he, "and you will find some-thing."

She did indeed find what she desired. But when the brother showed it to Father Rector, the latter told him that he must make of it two veils instead of one. The poor brother had measured carefully and knew that the piece was not enough for two. And yet Father Cajone insisted: "You must make two out of it. It is for you to see to it." Gerard returned to his workroom, measured it again, turned it this way and that, but all to no purpose; the piece was evidently too short. The Abbé Donato Spicci, a witness of the brother's embarrassment, remarked: "No one is bound to what is impossible."

"As for me," replied the holy Redemptorist, "I must obey, and as it is for Our Lord, it is for Him to remedy the defect." Then he began to pray, after which, taking the scissors, he cut out two magnificent veils, each having two perfectly symmetrical flowers.

He attributed his miracles to obedience. When at Calitri, he was asked to visit a very eminent surgeon who was in a dying state. At first he refused, but on Father Margotta's order, he went to the sick man, made over him the Sign of the Cross and instantly restored him to health. All present exclaimed: "A miracle!" But Gerard said humbly: "Behold what obedience can do."

A prominent man of the same city, who had a sister who was a religious, lay at the point of death. Father Margotta, moved by the distress of the good sister, ordered Gerard to pay the sick man a visit.

The Saint went, made upon his forehead the usual Sign of the Cross and thus recalled him from the gates of the tomb. The invalid made a good Confession and soon regained perfect health. Two ladies met him one day in Naples. One of them said to him, weeping: "My dear Brother, come, I beg you, and cure my poor daughter." Gerard at first refused, but at last, touched by the mother's tears, he said: "Yes, I will go. But I must first get permission." The Saint of Obedience would perform the miracle only by obedience.

15. HIS PATIENCE

GERARD had adopted for his maxim these words: "I wish to suffer everything to become a Saint." God, who wished to purify his virtue, took him at his word and made him pass through the most painful trial to which a just soul can be subjected.

To prepare His servant for immolation, the Holy Spirit led him for some days into solitude. It was in 1754. Holy Week was about to begin, and with it a series of ecstasies and mortifications with which the disciple of Jesus Crucified nourished his incomparable fervor. What passed during those eight days of intimate communication with the Divine Master? Gerard revealed it in a letter written at the time: "I have spent these days in infinite consolation of spirit." God prepared him by an abundance of heavenly delights for the abundance of humiliation that awaited him.

A short time after, St. Gerard was made the victim of an atrocious calumny, invented with cunning so diabolical that his superiors themselves knew not whether they ought to believe the accusation or not. St. Alphonsus, though suspending his judgment, took advantage of the occasion to test the virtue of the angelic religious. He called him to Nocera and laid before him the enormity of the supposed crime. Edification seemed to demand of Gerard self-justification, but he, harkening only to the inspiration of his humility, cast down his eyes and kept silence. He even accepted without reply the penance imposed on him, which consisted in privation of Communion and the severe prohibition of having any relations with the outside world. Despite this, he continued to regard St. Alphonsus with the most affectionate veneration. One day, when passing him, he was heard to exclaim: "O dear Father, you have the face of an Angel! When I see you, I am filled with consolation!"

The calumny made a great sensation in the convent, but the serenity of Gerard's countenance made a still greater impression. When urged to justify himself, he would say: "There is a God. It is for Him to see to it." "My cause is Thy cause," he would say to Our Lord. "If Thou dost will me to be humbled, I will it also, for Thou hast taught me to walk in the way of humiliation." He redoubled his austerities, retrenched his short sleep and very frequently passed the night in the open air on the roof. There, contemplating the starry firmament in which was reflected the divine power, he drew from the Heart of God the strength to support the most inexpressible trials. Then he took a little rest, lying in the coffin that had once held the precious remains of Father Sportelli, who had died in the odor of sanctity four years previously. His vengeance against his detractors consisted in begging Our Lord to deliver them from the sad state of sin in which they were living.

The holy Redemptorist's greatest affliction was caused not so much by seeing himself defamed in the eyes of his brethren and of the world, but by being deprived of Holy Communion. But even in this point, he submitted to the divine Will. To those that condoled with him he would say: "It is sufficient for me to have my Jesus in my heart." One day, when some were earnestly pressing him to ask St. Alphonsus the favor of approaching the Holy Table, he replied: "No, No!" And striking the baluster of the staircase with his hand, he added: "I want to die under the winepress of the Will of God." Another time, a priest asking him to serve his Mass, he replied: "Do not tempt me, for I would snatch Him from your hands at the altar." He alluded to the Sacred Host, for which he was famishing more than ever.

His delight at this time consisted in meditating on the divine perfections. It was in that vast ocean that he appeased his thirst for Holy Communion. He was asked one day how he could live without Communion. "I recreate myself," he responded, "in

the immensity of God." He seemed in truth always
plunged in the most sublime contemplation. Father
Cajone was witness to one of his ecstasies at this
time.

"Brother Gerard," the priest related, "fell sick,
and I was assisting as prefect of the sick. One
evening I was offering prayer with him, and I had
chosen for the subject of meditation the love of God
for us and the love that we ought to have for Him.
Scarcely had I mentioned these points when Gerard
was transported out of himself. He was lying on his
back, his head supported against the wall and his
eyes turned toward Heaven. I did not at first take
it for an ecstasy, but the meditation being finished,
I made a noise, but the brother remained in the same
attitude, his eyes immovable. The sight impressed
me deeply."

During this sickness St. Alphonsus, being in the
refectory one day, mentally ordered him to come at
once to him. Instantly Gerard, half-clothed, presented
himself before him. The Saint reproved him for the
impropriety of his appearance and demanded an
explanation. "I came at once," he replied modestly,
"because Your Reverence called me." The holy
Founder had in this a manifest proof of the perfect
obedience of his disciple and of the admirable privilege granted him of knowing supernaturally the will
of his superiors. Some days later, he sent Gerard to
Ciorani.

From Ciorani, where he remained but ten days,
our good brother was recalled to Nocera. He left in

this house a souvenir of his profound respect for the
Blessed Sacrament. One morning Holy Communion
was being carried to a sick man when it so happened that, on the way, the Sacred Host was lost.
Great was the distress of the priest who was carrying It and of the brothers who accompanied him.
They began to search for It in every direction, Gerard
among the rest. It was, say the witnesses, a touching sight to see him in his lively faith and in the
ardor of his love for Jesus Christ, whom he had not
received for a month—to see him, I say, ravished in
some way out of himself, his arms extended, seeking his Well-Beloved veiled under the Host. It was
he, in fact, who found It, and the joy that he felt
cannot be described. He was soon after sent to
Caposele, where there took place, a few days after
his arrival, the miracle of invisibility which we shall
relate further on.

It was now two months since the humble religious
had been placed in the crucible of tribulation, and
Our Lord, judging his trial sufficient, willed Himself
to justify him. The holy Founder received a letter
which filled him with joy. It emanated from the same
source as the calumny and formally declared before
God that the first letter was a tissue of falsehoods.

There was universal joy at this news. The Superior
General hastened to call the good brother to Nocera
and asked him why he had not justified himself.
"How could I do so," answered the humble religious,
"since the Rule orders us not to excuse ourselves?"
"Yes," returned St. Alphonsus, very much affected.

"Go, my son, and may God bless you! You are no doubt very sad at not being able to communicate?" "Not at all," answered Gerard. "If Jesus Christ willed not to come to me, how could I be dissatisfied?"

Up to this time, St. Alphonsus had had no special knowledge of Brother Gerard, who had always been attached to the convent of Iliceto. But Father Margotta, just at that time passing through Nocera, made known to the holy Founder the rare virtues of this good brother, the favors that he received from Heaven and the ardor with which he aspired to perfection. It was on this occasion that the Saint pronounced this magnificent eulogium: "If Brother Gerard had no other virtues than those he has practiced in this painful trial, they would suffice to give me the highest idea of his sanctity." Father Margotta, before starting for Naples, expressed the desire to have Gerard for a companion, as we have already said, and the favor was granted.

16. HIS ZEAL FOR SOULS

TO love Jesus Christ is to love the souls redeemed by the Blood of Jesus Christ. We can, then, judge of Gerard's zeal for the salvation of souls by the seraphic ardor that consumed him for our Divine Saviour.

In his resolutions, we read the following beautiful words: "O my God, may I convert as many sinners, if they exist, as there are grains of sand on the earth, drops of water in the ocean, leaves on the trees and stars in the firmament! I desire that all my prayers, Communions and good works may contribute to the conversion of poor sinners, and for that end I offer to God my life with the Precious Blood of Jesus Christ."

At the sight of the wonders of his zeal, his companions knew not how to express their admiration. "When he arrived in any place," they tell us, "his visit was equal to a mission. His presence was equivalent to that of several missionaries."

"Astonishing thing!" exclaimed Father Cafaro; "wherever that brother goes, he rouses the whole country."

"I have heard," wrote the Bishop of Melfi, "the great things he has done at Corato. I see more clearly than ever that Gerard is really a Saint, and I want to have him."

His appearance, the mere sight of him, say witnesses, was a sermon. One felt God in him. His burning words aroused in souls horror for sin, ardor for prayer, the love of Jesus and Mary and fidelity to the duties of their state. His good example, his prayers, his exhortations and his penances contributed greatly to the success of the Missions.

Gerard possessed special tact for inculcating the holy love of God and works of piety in children. His lessons remained forever engraved on their young souls. He had the habit of ending his lessons with the words: "So it is understood, we give ourselves entirely to the good God." Then, giving to every one a picture, or making the Sign of the Cross on the forehead, he sent them away full of joy to their parents.

He knew no greater happiness than to instruct the poor, the sick and souls most abandoned. It was sufficient to be poor, sick or miserable to receive from him the most sincere marks of tenderness. There exhaled from his person something divine, I know not what, which comforted hearts, cured souls and attracted them to virtue.

Although he was not a priest and consequently did not exercise the ministry of preaching, he had received from God a heavenly talent for the conversion of sinners. Father Tannoia, who had lived with him, said: "In all the missions at which Gerard assisted in the service of the priests, he effected numberless conversions. He kept the missionaries busy absolving penitents whom he in his humility had disposed for the Sacrament. Sometimes he used to say: 'I am sending you a big fish, and I hope it will not be disagreeable to you.' " That writer did not hesitate to call him "a hunter of souls—a hunter who had his eye always fixed on some prey for Jesus Christ."

To reach his ends, he used neither stratagem nor roundabout ways. He attacked vice boldly, weapon in hand. Sometimes, he sought in their own homes those that he wished to convert; sometimes, urged by an interior movement of the Holy Ghost, he would wait for them in the public street and insinuate himself into their heart in order to acquire the right to penetrate into their conscience. When he had suc-

ceeded in touching them, he showed them the sad
state of their souls and ended by gaining them to
Jesus Christ. When gentleness failed, he assumed a
stern manner. He knew how to terrify the sinner by
the tone of his voice. It was a common saying that
he had only to cast his eyes on a sinner to lead him
to penance. A great prelate once said, "It is God who
speaks by his lips."

The conversion of a soul was the only treasure
he sought. One day, when returning from a journey,
he met at a short distance from Iliceto an adventurer
who, noticing his shabby mantle, cassock and hat,
took him for a magician. He said to him: "If you
are looking for a treasure, here it is, ready to go
with you and help you."

"But," responded Gerard, "are you a man of
courage?"

"Ah!" answered the wretched man, "You do not
know who I am! I will tell you."

Thereupon he recounted his sad life, adding that
for many years, he had lived far from the Sacraments.
"Indeed," said Gerard, "I am going then to hunt a
treasure for you. This has been a happy meeting for
me. The treasure is as good as found."

They entered together the wood that lay on their
route. When they had reached a densely shaded spot,
Gerard mysteriously spread his mantle on the ground,
and making the sinner kneel on it, his hands joined,
he thus addressed him: "I have promised you a treasure, and I am going to keep my word," and he held
up his Crucifix. "Behold," said he, "the treasure that

you have lost for so many years!" Then he depicted the sad state of the man's poor soul and urged him to return to God. The sinner, touched by grace, began to weep, thanking God that he had permitted him to meet a Saint. Needless to say, he went forthwith to lay the burden of his sins at the feet of a confessor in our church of Iliceto.

"I would give my life a thousand times," said Gerard, "that God might not be offended." Sin of whatever kind froze him with horror, but of all sins, blasphemy was one of the most revolting to him. One day at Bovino he heard a carter blaspheming like a demon because his team could not disengage themselves from a rut in the road.

"Unhappy man! Stop blaspheming," cried the holy brother in a voice of thunder.

"Yes, I will stop," retorted the other, "if you get my wagon out of this rut. My mules will be killed."

Then Gerard, making the Sign of the Cross over the beasts, addressed them: "Creatures of God, in the name of the Most Holy Trinity, I order you to go on!" Instantly the team began to move and soon cleared the muddy rut. After remonstrating with the blasphemer, Gerard gave him his handkerchief, promising that under similar circumstances, by throwing it on the wagon, Heaven would come to his aid. The muleteer made happy experience of this promise.

Gerard abhorred injustice. One day he was having his horse shod by a farrier of San Menna. When the work was finished, the smith demanded exorbitant pay. The brother, incensed at the injustice, ordered his beast to give back the shoes. Instantly the animal shook his legs, and the shoes fell to the ground. As for Gerard, he went on his way, to the great amazement of the smith, who called him back, but in vain.

Another sin that deeply wounded the heart of the pious Redemptorist was sacrilege. He would have wished to extirpate it from the world. Jesus Christ favored the holy zeal that devoured him by revealing to him the secrets of consciences. A woman named Teresa Morante wished one day in Gerard's presence to make a show of sanctity, which she was far from possessing. The brother listened in silence to her beautiful words of piety. When she had finished, he said to her in a grave tone: "My daughter, why do you want to make me believe that? For years you have made sacrilegious Confessions and Communions, and now you are playing the Saint. Go make a good Confession, if you would not be damned." The woman, exceedingly abashed, went and threw herself at the feet of Canon Rossi, to whom she acknowledged that for ten years she had through shame been living in sacrilege. Then she made a general Confession with such contrition that she desired her sins to be made public in the biography of the holy brother to whom she owed her conversion.

A man of good position also had lived for years in sacrilege. Being alone with him one day, Gerard thus addressed him: "My son, you are living in sin.

Do you wish to die a reprobate? Confess the sin that you have for so long hidden and return to the grace of God." These words were sufficient. The sinner put an end to his profanations. An unfortunate woman was in the same dreadful state. "Dear sister," said Gerard to her one day, "how can you be at peace while living in disgrace with God? Why do you not confess that sin which you have passed over in silence for so many years?" Stupefied at the revelation, the sinner hastened to make a humble avowal of the state of her conscience.

Seeing a young girl leaving the church one day, the servant of God addressed her. "For what did you come here?" he asked.

"To go to Confession," she answered.

"I know," replied Gerard, "but you have not made a good Confession." Then he told her the sins that shame had led her to hide from the confessor. The poor girl, very much taken aback, returned immediately and was reconciled to God.

Gerard's zeal knew no bounds when there was a question of a sinner at the moment of death. A man named Liguoro was attacked by a sudden sickness which reduced him to the last extremity. For many years, he had not fulfilled the duties of religion. Seeing him at the point of death, his afflicted family implored Gerard to come quickly to the dying man. The zealous Redemptorist arrived without delay and, like another Elias, placed his mouth on that of the sick man. At the same instant the latter returned to consciousness and in the most

Christian manner received the Last Sacraments.

What zeal the holy brother employed for the reconciliation of enemies! A notary of Castelgrande had in a dispute killed the son of a man named Marco Carusi. The family of the victim conceived implacable hatred against the murderer, and every effort to reconcile them was unavailing. As this enmity might have fatal consequences, it was resolved to employ Brother Gerard's mediation. The servant of God first had a private interview with Marco, who was so impressed by the words of charity which came straight from his heart that he showed himself disposed to trample underfoot every desire of revenge. In the meantime, the holy brother was obliged to go to Muro for several days.

On his return, he found his work undone. Hell had made use of the mother of the victim to rekindle the flame. When the subject of reconciliation was broached, the wife flew into a violent rage, ran to her husband, loading him with a thousand imprecations and, seizing the blood-stained garments of her murdered son, threw them in his face. "Look!" she cried with fury, "look at these bloody garments, and then go and be reconciled if you can." These words roused in the husband's heart hatred stronger than ever.

When Gerard heard of it, he exclaimed: "No, no! Hell shall not triumph! God will have the victory!" Going to Carusi's house, crucifix in hand, he addressed the couple: "Come, come, tread underfoot this crucifix! Come on, tread underfoot the image of Him who pardoned His executioners. . . . You must pardon! When I first came here, it was in obedience to the call of man, but it is God Himself who sends me today. Listen, father and mother, who refuse to pardon! Your son is in Purgatory, and there he will remain as long as your resentment lasts. If you wish to deliver him, you must first be reconciled and then have five Masses celebrated for the repose of his soul. This is all that I have to say to you on the part of God. If you refuse, the most terrible chastisements await you." At these burning words the parents, conquered, exclaimed: "Yes, yes, we will forgive!" From that day, the two families were reconciled and, what is more wonderful, vowed sincere friendship.

—Part Four—

THE SUPERNATURAL GIFTS OF ST. GERARD MAJELLA

1. HIS ECSTASIES

IT would seem that God willed to renew in the person of our seraphic brother all the favors of the mystical order granted to other Saints. We shall consider them without returning to facts already mentioned, since mystical phenomena superabound in the life of this admirable servant of God.

When the soul is so absorbed in God that the exercise of the senses is suspended, we say that it is in ecstasy. Ecstasy is born of love. It is a delicious elevation of the soul toward a supernatural vision which charms and captivates by its goodness and beauty. The soul is then so fascinated by what it sees that it loses sight of the things of earth, forgets even itself, to behold no longer and to desire no longer anything but what is ravishing it. From Gerard's love for God sprang an intimacy with the Lord so close that his ecstasies began in his infancy. Few Saints were possessed of this gift with the continuousness such as we behold in Gerard. He seemed to live in a heavenly element. To be rapt in ecstasy, it was sufficient for him to think of the perfections of God, to contemplate the mystery of the Most Holy Trinity or that of the Incarnation, to cast his eyes upon a crucifix or a picture of the Blessed Virgin, to be in the presence of the Blessed Sacrament or of some wonder of creation. We have already in the course of this narrative mentioned so many of his raptures that we shall here confine ourselves to the following:

Gerard, intending to spend some days at Oliveto, received hospitality at the house of the archpriest Don Salvadore. One morning, Holy Mass was about to begin, and Gerard, who desired to communicate at it, did not appear. They called him, they knocked at his door, but there was no answer. At last they entered and found the seraphic brother kneeling in ecstasy, a crucifix in his right hand, the left hand laid on his breast, his face pale, his eyes half-closed. For more than half an hour, the household of the archpriest gazed in admiration at the ravishing spectacle.

This hospitable home had already been witness of a still more remarkable ecstasy, in which the servant of God was suspended without support in the air. It had taken place on the very morning of his arrival at Oliveto. Gerard had withdrawn to his room to pray. At the dinner hour, the archpriest went himself to invite him to dinner. But to his astonishment he found the brother ravished in ecstasy and raised about three feet from the ground. Filled with amazement, he withdrew, but returning shortly after, he found him in the same state. The whole household, far from sitting down to dinner, awaited the guest with tears of emotion. At last he appeared, his face all inflamed. "Please do not wait for me," said he to the archpriest. "I do not wish to inconvenience you." To preserve the memory of this rapture, the archpriest marked on the wall of the room the height to which he had seen the Saint elevated.

A similar prodigy was seen by all the people at Corato. On Good Friday, 1753, a picture representing Jesus Christ Crucified was carried in procession. When the procession entered the church of the Benedictines, Gerard was already inside engaged in prayer. As soon as he perceived the sacred image of the Saviour, an ecstatic transport seized him, and before the eyes of all, he was elevated to a considerable height from the ground, his eyes fixed on the picture.

There lived in Caposele a blind beggar who played most charmingly on the flute. Seeing him one day at the gate of the convent, Gerard begged him to play a well-known Italian air: "In all things, O my God, I wish Thy good pleasure, not my own." Immediately, a rapture of divine love seized upon the holy religious, and he began to leap, repeating the words: "Thy good pleasure, O my God, and not mine!" Then, suddenly raising his eyes toward Heaven, he was elevated in the air with the swiftness of an arrow, and there remained for some time ravished in ecstasy.

This reversal of the laws of gravity, this supernatural agility, took the shape even of an ecstatic flight. Gerard was returning one day to Iliceto with two young companions. As they were passing before a chapel dedicated to the Blessed Virgin, he turned the conversation to that tender and compassionate Mother. Then he took a pencil and wrote, I know not what, on a scrap of paper, which he tossed up in the air as if it were a letter. At the same moment, his two companions beheld him rise in the air and fly with the rapidity and lightness of a bird to a distance of over three quarters of a mile. Afterwards, they never ceased to recount this prodigious fact of which they had been witnesses.

But that was not the only time that the servant of God was favored with ecstatic flight. A pious person named Rosaria loved to relate that she had seen him one day carried up like a feather through the air, his arms extended. He flew thus for over three quarters of a mile, hastening to the convent to which he was called, no doubt, by some exercise of Rule or some desire of the Superior.

Divine love, being the source of spiritual joy, sometimes inundates the soul with floods of joy so marvelous that it appears on the body in various ways. Most frequently, it is a kind of intoxication, which—quickening the pulsations of the heart and filling it with extreme ardor and sweetness—makes it faint away. In this state, the soul utters sighs to relieve its delicious torments of love. In the last months of his life, our seraphic Redemptorist sometimes heaved such sighs as to attract upon himself looks of astonishment. Father Cajone reproved him for this singularity, at which Gerard, for his only reply, took the Father's hand and laid it upon his heart. The beating was so violent that the Father asked how it was possible for him to endure it and live? "Were I alone on a mountain," said Gerard one day to Dr. Santorelli, "it seems to me that I would set fire to the world with my flames of love." Then the holy religious placed the doctor's hand on his heart, which was beating with unheard-of impetuosity, as if trying to escape from his breast.

As David danced before the Ark of the Lord until he was looked upon as a fool, so do we behold Gerard, in the sublime emotions of his love, manifesting his joy by the holy folly of dancing. One day at Melfi, when in company with three of the Fathers, accompanying himself on the piano, he began to sing his favorite canticle: "If you wish to see God," etc. But soon, in a transport of love and ecstatic ravishment, he seized Father Stefano di Liguori and began to dance, wheeling him around hither and thither without the least effort, as if he had been a feather.

There occurred at Caposele one day an interesting contest between Brother Gerard and Father Strina, a man very devoted to the Infant Jesus: Gerard said to him playfully, "*You* do not love the Infant Jesus."

"And *you*," retorted the priest, "do not love the Madonna." Instantly, Gerard, wounded by love, seized Father Strina and, in an ecstatic transport, danced him around like a piece of straw.

God is a consuming fire. When He enters a soul, He inflames it, and its affections become sometimes so intense that they appear even on the body. One day, when the Seraph of Caposele was speaking of the love of Our Lord before the Dominican nuns of Corato, his face became suddenly radiant, his eyes fixed on Heaven. His hands grasping the bars of the grate, he heaved deep sighs and appeared ready to succumb under the flood of celestial emotions inundating his soul. He remained a long time in this state. At last, returning to himself, he called for cold water, of which he swallowed a few mouthfuls; then withdrawing, he bathed his breast to temper the heat of divine love.

A still more astonishing phenomenon took place at the Carmel of Ripacandida, a phenomenon called by mystics the "conflagration." In an ecstasy like that which we have just described, the body of our Seraph became luminous as the sun and incandescent to such a degree that the iron grate with its ornamental points bent under his hands like soft wax.

On another occasion, having fallen into ecstasy, he became so inflamed that rays of light shot from all parts of his person, and the parlor in which he was appeared to be on fire.

The restoration of fallen man is realized only by suffering. It was by suffering that Jesus Christ repaired the glory of God and redeemed man. This reparation and this redemption He continues in holy souls by suffering. Gerard had the honor of being called to reproduce in himself the expiatory life of the Divine Repairer. His love urged him to unite himself to the sufferings of his Well-Beloved. Could he fail to suffer on beholding the Object of his love despised, rejected, outraged? The same love that excited jubilation in his soul produced also suffering. It was by suffering that he became, like his Father, St. Alphonsus, the ideal of a Redemptorist, namely, of a religious destined by his sublime vocation to save souls by prayer, labor and suffering.

Thus is explained the powerful attraction that Gerard had for a crucified life. We have seen the thirst for suffering that devoured him and how often he sought to reproduce in his own flesh the various pains of the Passion. This ardent desire was so pleasing to the Divine Master that He deigned to favor the holy Brother with a grace granted only to a small number of His servants, such as St. Francis of Assisi and St. Catherine of Siena. Gerard asked for the favor of being able, like them, to experience the sufferings of Jesus Christ in His Passion, and he obtained it.

Every Friday, and still more especially on Good Friday, although he may have been perfectly well on the preceding days, he was seen crushed, as it were, under suffering and so weak that one might think him in agony. Several times on these days he vomited blood, and the night was spent in struggles with the demons, who tortured his body. His interior pains, his agony, his abandonment were inexpressible. His torments were like those that drew from the Saviour that cry of distress: "My God, My

God, why hast Thou forsaken Me?" And yet, the next day, Saturday, by a new prodigy, he was in a condition to attend to his occupations.

2. HIS INFUSED KNOWLEDGE

GOD is truth and light. When He enters our soul, He brings with Him knowledge unknown to reason. A pure soul, raised by sacrifice to the heights of the perfect life, frequently understands more about religion and its sublime mysteries than do theologians. This infused knowledge, which was given to our first parents before their sin, was also largely accorded to Gerard's pure and humble soul. God shed light on his understanding and gave to his lips the grace to communicate it. This supernatural knowledge drew around him many disciples and admirers.

Father Tannoia says: "Distinguished theologians—seculars and regulars—had recourse to his lights, to consult him on the direction of souls and to submit to him their difficulties. And Gerard, as if he had been a master in theology, discussed ascetic and moral questions profoundly. He solved doubts with the calmness and wisdom of a doctor, so that all who consulted him withdrew, wondering and saying: 'O Father, Lord of Heaven and earth, Thou hast hidden these things from the wise and prudent and hast revealed them to little ones.' "

The Bishop of Muro, Msgr. Vito Muio, expressed his admiration at the clearness and decision with which Gerard settled cases of conscience. Msgr.

Basta, Bishop of Melfi, became his disciple. Priests came in crowds to submit to him their doubts, for he seemed to be appointed a universal director of souls. He gave to all with astonishing aptness wise and lucid rules. Mgr. Amato, Bishop of Lacedonia, placed himself under his direction and followed his counsels with perfect docility, both in affairs appertaining to his diocese and to his personal conduct. "To speak with this good brother," he used to say, "on theological and spiritual matters is to become his disciple, so great are the lights one receives from him."

Thanks to the counsel of this lover of Christ, innumerable priests and laymen devoted themselves to prayer and the practice of virtue. Even souls consecrated to God in the cloister eagerly sought his spiritual instruction and had recourse to him as to an oracle for direction in the way of the most sublime perfection. This illiterate brother enjoyed such a reputation for his knowledge of doctrine that he attracted around him a crowd of learned men.

"I was one day in our convent at Naples," says Father de Robertis, "when there came an ecclesiastic who, drawn by Gerard's reputation, wished to confer with him on the mystery of the Most Holy Trinity, which he was then studying. He touched successively on the most difficult points, such as the generation of the Word, His co-eternity with the Father and the procession of the Holy Spirit. Far from appearing transported onto unknown ground, Gerard replied to every difficulty in a manner most precise and with surprising facility."

"The sages of the world," wrote Canon Bozzio, "are silent in the presence of this poor brother, who has never had any instruction. He draws his knowledge from its source, the Heart of Jesus, and not from the muddy cisterns of the human mind. In his mouth the most obscure mysteries become luminous."

"When Gerard spoke of divine things," says Dr. Santorelli, "he rose above himself. His word rendered the most difficult things intelligible, and what appeared obscure became clear on his lips. His conversations filled me with admiration, and I cannot conceive how a lowly brother could have penetrated so deeply into mysteries so sublime."

The archpriest of Lucia heard him explain in so luminous a manner the mysteries of the Holy Trinity and the Incarnation that neither St. Augustine nor St. Thomas, as he said in his enthusiasm, could have done better.

A young priest of Muro, proud of his theological knowledge, wished to try his strength with Gerard. But the latter pressed him so hard upon points of doctrine that, to his shame, he had to resort to silence. Then Gerard said to him: "Confess that one is not a theologian for having studied theology. True science is acquired only by humility and prayer."

The President of the Grand Seminary of Muro, desirous of showing his colleagues and the seminarians the gift of knowledge possessed by Gerard, begged the humble brother to explain before them these deep words of St. John: "In the beginning was the Word, and the Word was with God, and the Word was God." Gerard obeyed with childlike simplicity, explaining the generation of the Word in a manner so sublime that his hearers marveled.

"One conversation with this brother," said the Bishop of Muro, "does more good than a whole course of Lenten sermons."

"It is God who speaks by his lips," said a great prelate. "When he speaks, we are forced to listen; and when we hear him, we must obey him."

"One cannot read his letters," said Father Cafaro, "without wonder, especially when we remember that they were written by a lay brother who, in his youth, hardly learned to read and write."

That without study a man should receive infused knowledge is doubtless a marvel, but that he should communicate it instantaneously and at his own pleasure to others is more marvelous still. This is what Gerard did.

Donato Spicci, a priest of Muro, having entered Gerard's chamber one day, found lying on the table a biography of the venerable Sister Mary Crucified. He began to read a passage treating of the state of solitude on Calvary.

"These things are not for you," said Gerard to him.

"Is it Hebrew, that one cannot understand it?" asked Spicci.

"Ah, well, read and explain to me what the servant of God says!" replied Gerard.

The good priest tried, but he soon became confused, for he understood nothing of what he read. The humble Redemptorist then made a Sign of the Cross on his forehead and said, "Now read." Spicci read, understood and began to explain with such facility that he was astonished at himself. Dr. Santorelli was present when this prodigy took place.

Another priest, not being able to understand several passages of a book of Venerable Palafox, had recourse to Gerard. The latter made the Sign of the Cross on his forehead and said to him: "In the name of the Most Holy Trinity, now read." He read and found his mind so enlightened on the sense of those passages that he was able easily to explain them to others.

3. HIS SPIRIT OF PROPHECY

IT belongs only to God to know the future, and He is accustomed to reveal it only to souls of eminent virtue, either to declare their sanctity or for the good of others. They have, then, what we call the gift of prophecy.

Brother Gerard possessed this extraordinary light in a high degree. His first prophecy concerned himself. One day, when he had voluntarily delivered himself up to all the outrages of the young people of Muro, he exclaimed: "You despise me today, but the time will come when you will esteem it an honor to kiss my hand." Some years later, these words were literally realized. When the servant of God returned to his native city in the habit of a Redemptorist, rich and poor lavished on him marks of high veneration. Whenever he appeared on the street, crowds gathered around him, some to kiss his right hand, some his left.

He prophesied to a young professed student named Pietro Blasucci that he would one day be Superior General of the Institute. Forty years later, in 1793, the prophecy was realized.

One day he visited a young man of Melfi, Michaelo di Michele, who was lying dangerously ill. "What! You have fever?" he said, feeling his pulse. "Not at all, you are well." At the same moment, the sick man was cured. "Some day," said Gerard to him, "you will be one of ours." "I will be that," rejoined Michaelo, "when I can touch the sky with my hand." By these words, he expressed his deep repugnance to the religious life. However, Michaelo did become a Redemptorist and distinguished himself by his apostolic zeal.

A young man of fine worldly prospects ardently desired to enter our Institute, but he encountered serious difficulty on the part of the civil law. One day, he met the Saint traveling with a nobleman, and he began to follow him at a distance. Suddenly, Gerard turned back. "Be at peace," he said to the youth. "Before three months, you will be in our Congregation." The event confirmed the prophecy. This postulant became Father Negri, who had the ineffable happiness of receiving St. Alphonsus' last sigh.

One day when Gerard was showing the convent

to some strangers, they saw a runaway horse dashing with its rider toward a precipice. "He is lost!" exclaimed the bystanders in fright. "O holy Virgin, help him!" cried Gerard. Then, turning to his companions, he said: "He will fall, but he will not be injured." And this was in truth what happened.

A poor woman came one day to recommend to the servant of God her husband, who was at the point of death. "Do not fear," said he, "your husband will not die of this sickness, but he will not regain his health all at once. He will have to suffer a long time before he is in a condition to resume his occupations." The prophecy was accomplished to the letter.

A Carmelite nun of Ripacandida was about to die, but Gerard declared that she would recover.

"How can that be?" said the sisters to him, "for she is already in her agony."

"You will see that what I say is true," replied the brother. "The sick sister will live, for she still has to make progress in perfection." She in fact recovered and became one of the most fervent members of the community.

One day, being at the house of Carmin Petrone of Muro, he saw the child of the family, only three years old. "This child," said Gerard to the father, "will soon be taken from you. He will die with a musical instrument in his hand." The event turned out as Gerard had predicted.

"Sister," said Gerard to a religious of Foggia, "you frequently go to Confession, do you not? Happy you are! for the day of your death is near." Seeing that the religious, who was young and strong—as well as the community present—did not take his words seriously, he repeated: "Sister, keep very close to God, for in eight days you will no longer be alive." The eighth day found her in eternity as predicted.

Whenever Gerard went to Muro, a certain clock-maker entertained him in his own home. God willed to recompense this charity by saving his wife, who for a long time had been living in a state of sacrilege. Gerard revealed to her the sins that she had hidden and added: "Prepare for death by a good Confession, for soon you will appear before God." Shortly after, the woman, though robust, departed this life.

One day when he was going to Vietri, a woman of wicked life asked him for a picture of the Blessed Virgin. "Here is one," said Gerard, "but think of your soul and commend yourself earnestly to Mary, for you have only a few days to live." Three days after the prediction, the woman died, reconciled to God.

A wealthy man of Calitri, entirely taken up by the affairs of this world, was living in disgrace with God and forgetfulness of his own soul. Gerard visited him and invited him to make a retreat in the convent of Caposele. The man excused himself under frivolous pretexts, but Gerard insisted. "I will see about it in October," he said. "You will see about it in October, do you say?" responded the brother. "I declare to you that you will not see October." In the month of August, a malignant fever carried the worldling to the tomb.

In one of his rounds at Oliveto, Gerard, gazing fixedly upon a certain child, predicted that it would fall into great disorders. As the child increased in years, he became a monster of crime and vice. One day, when he was making an attempt on the life of his father, the latter killed him in self-defense.

At Muro, the Saint once passed by an impious fellow who was uttering execrable blasphemies against the Most Holy Trinity. Gerard shuddered with horror, and turning to the president of the seminary, who was with him, he said, "These blasphemies will not go unpunished. You will soon see!" Three days later, the unfortunate sinner was killed in the public square by a musket shot, without a moment to return to the grace of God.

A prophet for others, Gerard was also one for himself. Six months in advance, he predicted his own death.

"Doctor," he said one day in a joyous tone to Dr. Santorelli, "do you know that I shall die of consumption this year?"

"How do you know that?" asked the doctor.

"I have begged it as a favor from Our Lord, and He has promised me," answered Gerard.

"But why of consumption?" asked the doctor.

"Because dying of that sickness, I shall die abandoned, for though in the Community they have the greatest charity for the sick, yet for that kind of death, one cannot count on the presence of the nurses."

Some days before, he had said the same thing to Brother Januarius Rendina: "I have asked Jesus Christ the favor of dying of consumption and abandoned." He obtained both requests, as we shall see later on.

When leaving Oliveto, a month and a half before his death, the good Redemptorist went to take leave of the Pirofalo family. He said to them: "Look from time to time toward the convent of Caposele. As long as you see a strip of white linen at a window, you may know that I am alive, but when it disappears, I shall be no more." Oliveto is several miles from Caposele, but in spite of the distance, the linen was seen as long as Gerard lived, and it disappeared the very day he died.

4. HIS DISCERNMENT OF SPIRITS AND PENETRATION OF HEARTS

THE creature cannot know the secrets of hearts without light from God Himself, who alone sounds hearts and reins and whose eye nothing escapes. There are few Saints who have had this gift of discernment of spirits and penetration of hearts in the same degree as Brother Gerard.

A young man, a consumptive named Nicholas Benincasa, was often in the Saint's company. One day, when he was mentally admiring his virtues, he said to himself: "This good Brother Gerard performs so many miracles for others, and he does not pray God to take from me this lung trouble." He had

scarcely formulated the complaint in his heart when
the brother said to him: "What are you saying there?
You say I do not pray for you. Indeed I do. But God
does not wish to cure you. My son, you are not for
this world." The young man died shortly after and,
as the Saint's words signified, he went to a better
world.

Don Filippo Salvadore, going one day to the
Saint's room, found him in ecstasy before a crucifix and raised from the ground. He had come to ask
advice in some affair of conscience, but seeing how
things stood, he was about to withdraw when Gerard
said to him: "Don Filippo, I know why you have
come. Do not scruple such and such a thing. Confide
in Providence." These words were precisely the solu-
tion to all the questions that the good Christian
wished to put to the holy religious.

A lady of Lacedonia knew not how to break off
an attachment which was drawing her little by little toward the precipice. She opened her heart to
Gerard, who said to her: "Your fault, madam, is
that you are not sufficiently faithful to Jesus Christ."
Then he showed her how she was secretly cherish-
ing her passion. "Shut the door of your heart," he
said at the close of their interview, "and have confidence." The woman put in practice the advice of
the servant of God and was forever delivered from
her temptation.

Another woman, supposedly possessed, had wea-
ried the charity of several priests who for two months
had tried to banish the demon by holy exorcisms.

Gerard, after seeing her, declared that there was nothing of the kind the matter with her. "You act in this way for such and such a reason," he said to her. "Stop your antics, or to your shame I shall make known everything." The woman, thoroughly frightened, took good care never again to feign diabolical possession.

One day when Gerard was at San Gregorio at the house of the archpriest, a friend of the latter arrived unexpectedly. Abruptly changing the subject of conversation, the Saint proposed a certain case in morals. The archpriest could not understand what connection it had with the question under discussion. But the visitor drew him aside and said to him in surprise: "You have a Saint here. That case, just as Brother Gerard proposed it, happened to me only an instant ago. I make it known—to my shame and to the glory of the holy brother."

Gerard detested the sloth of those that pass themselves off for cripples in order to live on public charity. Once he saw one of these knaves who, dragging himself along on his crutches, one leg bandaged in old rags, was imploring alms from pious persons on the road leading to the convent. Indignant at such trickery, Gerard went straight up to him and, tearing off his bandages, exclaimed: "Cheat that you are, if you want to save your soul, cease to mock God and men!" Beholding his fraud discovered, the pretended cripple ran off on both legs, forgetful even of his crutches.

With the Sisters of San Salvatore at Foggia, there

was a little scholar named Gertrude de Cecilia. "My child," said Gerard to her one day, "you are thinking of going to Communion. But no, your Confession was not good. You omitted such and such a sin. Go back to your confessor and make a general Confession." Gertrude thought she would die of shame at this revelation. She made as good a general Confession as she possibly could, but soon she became scrupulous and melancholy. No one could guess the cause. One day, as Gerard was passing through Foggia, he sent for her and said: "Be at peace. Your Confession was well made." The child, reassured by these words, felt spring up in her heart a joy and peace till then unknown.

Once, when a general Communion was going on at Iliceto, Gerard ran down quickly from the gallery and hastened into the church. It was to remove quickly from the Holy Table a man who was on the point of making a sacrilegious Communion. He took him aside and showed him the crime he was going to commit. Filled with repentance, the sinner ran to throw himself at the feet of his confessor. On leaving the holy tribunal, he cried aloud: "I was ashamed to confess my sins to the priest, but Brother Gerard revealed them to me. Now to my own humiliation I wish to confess them to the whole world." He would indeed have done so had not a priest who was nearby prevented him.

The notary, De Robertis of Muro, had been guilty of murder. Many years had flown by, and the murderer remained unknown. The unhappy man had even concealed the crime in Confession. One day, Brother Gerard met him and, without preamble, said: "Your conscience is in a bad state. You have never confessed the murder that you committed under a cherry tree in your vineyard." This unexpected and precise revelation produced its effect. The notary made a sincere Confession. He feared not to divulge his sin, adding: "Yes, Gerard is a great Saint. He revealed to me what was known only to God and myself."

The following incident took place in Naples: Gerard and a priest named Collela happened to enter together the store of a dealer in articles of devotion. The dealer affected a sanctity that he was far from possessing. The holy Redemptorist, drawing him aside, told him of a grave sin that he had committed with God alone for witness. As soon as Gerard had left the store, the dealer could not help saying to Father Collela: "That Father must be a very great servant of God. I am quite disturbed. He revealed to me a sin which only God and myself knew."

Crossing the public square of Auletta one day, Gerard went straight up to a stranger and accosted him thus: "My son, how can you be in peace? On such and such a day, you committed such and such a sin, and you have not yet confessed it. Go at once to a priest, and be reconciled to God." The sinner fell on his knees, acknowledged his sin and hastened to make a sincere Confession to a priest.

A retreat was to be preached at the convent of Caposele. Knowing that some fugitive villagers were in the neighboring wood, Gerard invited them by letter to assist at the holy exercises. They came. The Saint sent them to Father Patrella to Confession. Meeting them shortly after, he asked: "Have you been to Confession?"

"Yes," they answered.

"A beautiful Confession you have made!" replied the brother. "And such and such a sin? Why have you not told them?"

These words stupefied them. "It is true," they said, "and since it is so, please come with us and whisper our sins in our ear, for we might not recall them all and thus deceive ourselves."

We have already cited so many facts which clearly prove that the holy brother had the gift of reading consciences that it would be superfluous to give others.

5. HIS VISION AT A DISTANCE

OUR holy brother was gifted also with divine light, by which he saw in spirit, even at a distance, what he could not know by natural means.

He read souls from afar. "Dear Sister," he wrote to Mother Mary of Jesus, "I know the trials through which you have passed. I understand them clearly, distinctly. I see them more clearly than you do yourself." Some time after, he again wrote: "It is useless for you to explain to me your troubles. I know them, I see them in God."

He saw events at a distance. One day at Naples,

he met a young fellow townsman. "My dear Pascal," he said to him with emotion, "do you know that our archpriest has just been assassinated in one of the streets of Muro?"

"Impossible!" exclaimed the other in amazement. "I have only this moment received a letter from Muro, and no mention is made of the fact."

"And yet it is so, my friend. There is no doubt about it." The assassination had really taken place, but so recently that it would have been impossible for the news to travel so quickly some sixty miles' distance.

Canon Rossi went to spend some days of solitude at Caposele; during this time, there happened unexpectedly at Melfi, his native city, an event of great importance, on account of which he had to send there a special messenger. As the latter delayed his return, the canon, who was at the time alone in a retired corner of the garden, began to experience great anxiety. Gerard, however, was supernaturally aware both of the canon's agitation and of the happy issue of the affair at hand. In his great charity, he went at once to him and said: "Be at peace, Reverend Father, all has gone well at Melfi, and just as you would have it." The messenger, returning soon after, confirmed the good news.

Once when about to pass through Oliveto, Gerard wrote to the archpriest Don Salvadore a letter in the following terms: "You have so long desired to know the sinner who is now writing to you. Behold your wishes are going to be gratified." These words greatly surprised the archpriest, who had indeed very much desired to know the holy Redemptorist, but who had never expressed his desire to anyone. On arriving, Gerard said to him: "Did you read the last words of my letter?"

Feigning not to understand the question, Don Salvadore answered: "Yes, I read the words, 'Your unworthy servant.'"

"Not that," replied Gerard.

"Well, I saw also, 'Your brother in Jesus Christ.'"

"Nor was it that," said Gerard.

"Well, what then?"

"I know that you have long desired to see me. Behold the Lord has sent me to you." Don Salvadore was convinced by this that Gerard was possessed of supernatural clairvoyance, and he ever after looked upon him as a Saint.

The servant of God knew even the secrets of the other life. One day when in company with his brethren at Iliceto, he suddenly fell into ecstasy. When asked the cause, he answered: "I have just seen the soul of Father Cafaro mounting to Heaven. His place is not far from that of St. Paul, because by his constant, zealous and fervent preaching, he gained many souls to Jesus Christ." It was precisely the day and the hour that the holy missionary gave up his soul to God in the convent of Caposele.

The Saint knew by revelation another cause of Father Cafaro's glory. One day, during the community recreation, the conversation ran on about the eminent virtues of that apostolic man. "Yes," said

Gerard, "Don Paul is a great Saint, and he rejoices in God not far from St. Paul because, like that Apostle, he was submitted to the trial of temptation." This was indeed true, but excepting one intimate friend, no one had any knowledge of Father Cafaro's interior martyrdom.

Gerard was favored with a similar vision relative to another Redemptorist. Three days before his death, at the noon recreation, he was suddenly ravished in ecstasy and was heard to exclaim joyfully: "See, see, our blessed Father Latessa going up to Paradise!"

On September 4, 1755, the countenance of our thaumaturgus expressed great emotion. Brother Stefano Sperduto asked him the reason. "My dear brother," he answered, "know that today the beautiful soul of Sister Maria Celestia has gone to Heaven. She has gone to reap the reward due to her great love for Jesus and Mary."

To a religious of Ripacandida, he wrote: "You tell me that Sister Oliviera sends me her greetings. It is true, but it is from the height of Heaven." The sister had, in truth, already left this land of exile.

A painter of Oliveto, a relative of Don Salvadore, went to Caposele for some work on the convent. When Gerard opened the door for him, he thus accosted the painter: "The archpriest is in grief. His father has just expired."

"Impossible!" exclaimed the painter. "I saw him today in good health." But Gerard assured him that he was dead of a stroke of apoplexy. "In that case," said the other, "I shall return to Oliveto to render him the last duties."

"Yes, go," responded the servant of God, "and tell the archpriest that he may rejoice, for his excellent father is in Heaven."

The holy brother's glance penetrated, as we have already seen, even into the depths of Purgatory. A girl of Lacedonia named Lella Cocchia was inconsolable over the death of her mother. One day, when Gerard was passing through the city, she begged him to tell her where her mother's soul was. "She is in Purgatory," replied the brother. "Offer forty Communions for her, and she will be delivered." Lella, urged by her filial love, followed the counsel and offered the forty Communions. Then her mother appeared to her, thanked her and told her that she was going to Heaven.

Even the secrets of Hell were unveiled to the divinely illumined eye of Gerard. A miserable man who had deceived the world under cover of a hermit's life was dying in our house of Iliceto. He had so loathsome a sickness that no one dared approach him. Brother Gerard lavished the tenderest cares upon him and prepared him for a holy death. But the unhappy man did not profit by the mercy of God. One day when Gerard was praying for the repose of his soul, the unfortunate reprobate appeared and in a frightful voice said to him: "Pray not for me. By a just judgment of God, I am damned." The good religious was so terrified by his horrible appearance that he never forgot it.

6. HIS BILOCATION

THERE exists a mystical phenomenon in the life of the Saints, the more astonishing because it is so rare, namely, that of bilocation. It happens when a person is found in two different places at one and the same time. One of the most celebrated facts of this kind and the best attested is that which happened to St. Alphonsus di Liguori. On the morning of September 20, 1774, this Bishop, contrary to his custom, after his Mass sank down in his armchair. "There," as we read in the documents of his canonization, "he experienced a kind of swoon, and for two days remained in a sweet and deep sleep. A servant wished to awaken him but his Vicar General, Don Nicholas de Rubino, ordered them to allow him to rest, though without losing sight of him. Having at last returned to consciousness, St. Alphonsus rang for his attendants, who hastily answered the summons. Seeing them very much astonished, he asked: 'What is the matter with you?' 'What is the matter with *us?*' they answered. 'For two days you have not spoken nor given any sign of life!' 'You thought me asleep,' replied the servant of God, 'but it was not so. I went to assist the Pope, who was dying.' They soon learned in truth about the death of Clement XIV, which happened on September 22, about eight in the morning, that is, at the very moment that the Saint had rung the little bell."

The advocate of the cause adds: "The coincidence of the day on which Alphonsus was ravished in ecstasy with that of the death of the Sovereign Pontiff and the precision with which he declared at Arienzo, at the very hour of the event, that the Holy Father had ceased to live are unquestionable arguments which prove the truth of the marvelous favor granted to our Saint and also to the dying Pontiff." (*Vie de saint Alphonse,* by Mgr. Dupanloup, Ch. XXV).

Brother Gerard was favored several times in his life with this extraordinary gift of bilocation.

One day when he had received no answer from Muro upon some pressing affairs concerning the glory of God, he said: "I must go there today." The next day, indeed, he was seen at Muro, while on the other hand they declared that he had not quitted his own convent.

Another day, Father Margotta said to Dr. Santorelli: "Do you not know that Gerard, although in his room, spent the night in ecstasy before the Most Blessed Sacrament in the choir of the Franciscans?"

Similar prodigies were frequently repeated. Many a time, although without leaving the house, he was seen at Caposele visiting the sick! "One day among others," says Dr. Santorelli, "while I was visiting my sick, I felt everywhere I went Brother Gerard at my side, just as really as if I had seen him before my eyes. After my rounds, I went to the convent and, meeting the brother, I said to him: 'What did you want with me all day long, following me everywhere?'

"'What did I want?' he answered. 'Do you not know that I have to go away tomorrow? I wanted to visit all my dear sick.'"

Nicholo Fiore, archpriest of Teora, impressed by Gerard's high reputation, was very anxious to make his acquaintance, and he manifested his desire to Dr. Santorelli. The latter spoke of it to the brother, who replied: "I am willing to gratify it. I shall go see him." A few days after, the archpriest came to the convent to visit the Archbishop of Conza. Dr. Santorelli met him and said: "I am going to introduce Brother Gerard to you."

"It is not necessary," replied the archpriest, "he came to my house one evening. I know him. I am charmed by him."

Dr. Santorelli, who knew that the brother had not gone to Teora, took the archpriest to a place where Gerard was with the other brothers and said to him: "Let us see, which is Brother Gerard?" The archpriest pointed him out at once.

A domestic of De Gregorio of Lacedonia was confined to bed with intolerable sufferings. One night he exclaimed: "O dear Brother Gerard, where are you? Why do you not come to help me?"

Instantly the charitable Redemptorist was at his side. "My son, here I am. I come to help you. Confide in God and be cured." Then he made the Sign of the Cross on the forehead of the sick man, who immediately arose perfectly cured.

Theodore Cleffi of Caposele, on his way home after a long conversation with Gerard, called on a very poor sick man. "I have need of nothing," said the poor man, "for Brother Gerard has just this moment left me after giving me all that I needed."

"That is not so," returned Cleffi, "for I have just left the brother after a long conversation with him." But the sick man declared that what he said was so and, as a proof of his words, showed what he had received from Gerard's charity.

Gerard promised the family of Dr. Santorelli to visit them on a certain evening. The doctor could not restrain a smile of incredulity. "I am not joking," said the brother. In fact, the doctor's sister saw the servant of God that same evening. She declared that she could swear to it, that it was not an effect of her imagination.

7. HIS POWER OVER NATURE

IT sometimes happens that Almighty God gives in part to His servants that empire over nature which the first man in his state of innocence possessed. The prodigies that Saints who were endowed with this gift operate have for their aim either the succor of their neighbor, the repression of evil or the signalizing of sanctity itself. It would seem that the Creator had placed all creation at Gerard's service.

One day on the road from Andria to Corato he met a farmer in great distress. Mice had ravaged the whole of the field that he had sown, and it was the only resource he had for the support of his family.

"Would you rather have them die or go else-where?" asked the brother, full of compassion.

"I would rather they would die," answered the peasant.

Gerard raised his hand, made the Sign of the Cross toward the devastated field, and at the same instant the ground was covered with dead and dying mice. At the sight of this prodigy, the farmer, beside himself with joy, ran to Corato exclaiming: "The Saint is here! The Saint is here!"

All Gerard had to do was to call the little birds, and they flew to light on his hand. A nephew of the archpriest Don Salvadore kept a little bird in a cage. After caressing it, Gerard set it at liberty. At the sight of his bird flying away, the child began to utter piercing cries. To quiet him, the good brother went to the window: "Come back," said he, "come back, for the child is weeping." Instantly, the bird returned and perched on the hand of the Saint, who gave it back to its owner.

One day at table in our convent of Caposele, Gerard, by a wave of the hand, called the birds that were warbling in the neighborhood. The charming little creatures, docile to the orders of him who so faithfully obeyed his God, came at once fluttering around the holy religious and hopping over the table in front of him. Their eyes were fixed on his, and they seemed to listen attentively to the words full of sweetness and simplicity that he addressed to them, as if they were endowed with intelligence.

The elements were also submissive to Gerard. He

was sent one day on an errand to Caposele. But hardly had he set out when the rain fell in torrents. The Father Rector at once dispatched a messenger to tell him to return. When the obedient religious entered the house, not a drop of rain had dampened his garments. He once performed the same miracle in favor of seven postulants whom he was bringing to the convent.

The following fact is still more marvelous: A father was one day taking his two daughters to a certain convent, and Gerard was showing them the way. Suddenly, a river swollen by the rains obstructed their path. At the command of the holy religious, behold, the waters divided, as formerly the Jordan at the voice of Josue, and, forming a double wall, allowed the travellers to pass over with dry feet.

The laws of gravity vanished before the will of this great servant of God. Passing through Senerchia, he found some of the inhabitants in great perplexity. They were not able to bring down from the neighboring mountain several huge chestnut trees, which they wanted to use in the erection of their parish church. Gerard, always ready to sympathize in the troubles of others, had them take him up the mountain. He found the trees to be of extraordinary size. Tying a rope to one of the largest, whose weight defied the efforts of oxen and buffaloes, he exclaimed: "Creature of God, in the name of the Most Holy Trinity, I order thee to follow me." Then, to the intense astonishment of the spectators, he alone drew it—and without effort—to the church. At the sight of this prodigy, the people courageously recommenced their labor, and soon all the trees were brought down the mountain.

At Naples Gerard performed a wonder of the same kind, and one even more marvelous in the presence of a multitude of witnesses. One day, when journeying along the seashore, he saw at some distance an immense crowd who were rending the air with their cries and lamentations. A furious tempest was raging, and they were watching with fright a vessel filled with passengers and which looked as if it might at any moment be swallowed up in the foaming waves. Moved to compassion, the servant of God made the Sign of the Cross over the furious waters, threw his mantle from his shoulders and, stepping into the waves, called out to the vessel: "In the name of the Most Holy Trinity, pause!" Then he laid hold of it and drew it like a floating cork to the shore, he himself walking through the waters without even getting his clothes wet. "A miracle!" "A miracle!" resounded on all sides. The enthusiasm was indescribable. They wanted to surround him and give him testimonies of veneration, but the humble brother fled toward the city as if he had committed some crime and took refuge in the house of a friend, which he did not leave until after dark.

"How were you able to draw the vessel?" asked Father Margotta.

"O Father," was the answer, "when God wills, everything is possible."

Questioned later by Father Cajone with respect to

the same prodigy, Gerard answered smilingly, "I caught it with two fingers, and drew it to shore. In the state in which I then was, I could have flown in the air."

The next day, Canon Bozzio, having come to Naples on business, visited his friend, and they went out together. They met an Abbé who, pointing out Gerard, said: "See, there is the man who yesterday cast himself into the waves." The brother, who was hoping not to be recognized, was quite annoyed and hastened his steps. The canon, not being able to follow him, cried out: "Wait for me, I beg you! Stop!" But Gerard only hurried on more quickly. To crown his misery, the beggars began to run after him, crying: "The Saint! The Saint! See the Saint!" But Gerard made his escape, and the canon learned from one of the beggars the event of the preceding day.

We read in the Lives of the Saints that there were some who possessed the gift of rendering themselves invisible to their fellowmen. This favor was not refused to our pious Redemptorist. Incessantly surrounded by priests and laymen, the good brother could find no time for recollection. He asked the Father Rector of Caposele permission to make a day's retreat, and the favor was granted. But even on that day of solitude, as the Father Rector had need of the good brother, he sent for him to his room, but he was not there. They looked in the choir, but no Brother Gerard could be seen. The whole house was searched, but he could not be found. In the midst of the search, Dr. Santorelli entered. The

Father Rector said to him earnestly: "We have lost Brother Gerard." The doctor smilingly answered: "Perhaps he is hiding. Let us go see." And taking a brother with him, he went around looking everywhere, but to no purpose. "Oh, never mind." he said. "When it is time for Communion, you will see him come out of his retreat." And so it happened. Our Seraph appeared exactly at that moment. Soon the Father Rector called him and inquired where he had been. "In my room," answered Gerard. "What! in your room," replied the Superior. "They looked for you there twice without finding you." Gerard smiled, but made no answer. Then receiving a command to explain what seemed so strange, he said simply: "Fearing to be distracted in my retreat, I asked Jesus Christ for the grace to become invisible." "I forgive you this once," said Father Rector, "but take care for the future not to make such requests." Now, Gerard's chamber did not measure ten feet square and contained only a poor bed and little table, without any furniture whatever that could prevent his being seen. "Where in the world were you?" Dr. Santorelli asked him. "How could you say that you were in your cell when I searched every nook and corner of it with Brother Nicolo and yet could not find you?" At these words, Gerard took the incredulous doctor by the arm, conducted him to his cell, and showed him where he had been sitting on a little stool near the door! "But we looked for you everywhere without seeing you," said the doctor. "Well," replied Gerard smiling, "it is because *sometimes* I make myself very little." This miracle was not long in being noised about Caposele. Even the children used to say when proposing a certain game of hide-and-seek, "Let us play Brother Gerard!" We must say here with the Royal Prophet that God is wonderful in His Saints and that He knows how to refuse nothing to their prayers.

Here are some marvels still more astonishing: The Berilli family of Calitri had sustained a heavy loss in the death of a fine mule. Gerard, having heard of their affliction, as an acknowledgment of the hospitality he had received at their house, asked to be taken to the stable. There the mule lay dead on the ground. Gerard made the Sign of the Cross over it, and at once the animal rose full of life, to the great joy and amazement of the beholders.

When speaking of Gerard's incomparable charity toward the poor, we have recorded the marvelous gift he possessed of multiplying food. We shall cite here the following facts: The humble brother did not blush to beg alms. One day, going into a little cottage, he asked the poor woman who dwelt there to give him a morsel of bread. "Alas!" she replied, "I have nothing but a handful of meal." "What! You have nothing, and this chest full of bread?" exclaimed Gerard. "It is empty," replied the woman. "Let us see, open it," said Gerard. Wonderful to relate, it was full of bread. The poor woman could not believe her eyes.

Our Brother Antonio of Cosimo, on the quest in the Basilicata, entered the house of a blind lady named Lucretia and told her the object of his visit. Instantly, the lady started forward, exclaiming: "O dear Brother Gerard, how glad I am to see you!"

"But I am not Brother Gerard," said Antonio. "He is dead several years."

"He is dead!" she exclaimed with a sigh. "Oh, what a great Saint he was!"

Then she told that, in a time of need, the compassionate brother had predicted to her that the only remaining bushel of meal would last a whole year, that is, till the next harvest. "Now," she continued, "that prophecy was accomplished to the letter. With that one bushel of meal, I was able for a year to feed not only my whole family, but all my workmen besides, and there even remained some over, which I sold for the other necessities of my family. The year following, on the anniversary of Brother Gerard's prophecy, the miraculous meal suddenly gave out. Oh, yes, Brother Gerard was a great Saint!"

We shall end this series of prodigies by one more which shows Gerard's power over the material world: Here we shall find objects damaged or broken restored to their original condition. During a mission at Calitri, the servant of God inadvertently let fall a large vessel of oil. It was at the house of the Berilli family, where the missionaries were staying. The vessel was broken to pieces and the oil ran over the floor. On seeing the accident, a daughter of the family began to reproach the brother, calling him stupid and awkward. Hearing the sound of her daughter's angry voice, Donna Berilli ran to see what was the matter. "It is nothing, my daughter," she said, "the oil will not be lost. I will gather it up with some wool." She went at once to get the wool, but when she reappeared, to her great surprise she beheld the vessel perfectly restored and with more oil in it than before the accident.

A widow, Victoria Bruno of Melfi, had sold a certain quantity of wine, but when the purchaser came to take possession, he found it spoiled. This of course cancelled the contract. Gerard, happening to call that day at the house, was informed of the loss of the wine. "Oh, that's nothing, that's nothing!" he said, and at the same time advised the distressed widow to put a little picture of the Immaculate Conception into the cask, and the wine would become good again. As Victoria hesitated to follow the counsel, the Saint said: "Is it you who will restore to the wine its good quality? No, it is God; therefore, do as I tell you." The woman obeyed, and the wine at once regained its excellence.

At the house of De Gregorio at Lacedonia, by the Sign of the Cross, Gerard also restored freshness to a cask of wine that had become sour.

8. HIS POWER OVER SICKNESS

ACCORDING to Gerard's contemporaries, the miraculous cures that he effected during his life are so numerous that it would take volumes to record them. God seemed to have appointed him the lieutenant of His own almighty power. No kind of infirmity resisted the voice of the new thaumaturgus. This we have already proved in preceding pages. We shall now cite some other facts.

A little girl of Auletta, a cripple from her birth, had no power of movement. Gerard was begged to recommend her to God. "But this child is cured," he replied. So saying, he called her, and to the great surprise of the bystanders, the child sprang from her bed and ran to kiss the hand of her benefactor. While those present cried: "A miracle! A miracle!" Gerard, quite disconcerted, ran to hide in the house of a priest named Abondati. But they followed him, crying: "The Saint! The Saint!" The good brother, frightened, stole away by a rear entrance. Several years after, as Brother Francesco Fiore was passing through Auletta, they pointed out to him the girl, saying: "See, this is the one whom Brother Gerard cured."

A mother came one day to present to him a child whose lower limbs were deformed. Scarcely had he touched the child's limbs when they were restored.

A stranger who happened to be in our convent of Caposele was suddenly attacked by violent sciatic pains. What distressed him above all was to see himself reduced to so sad a state away from home. Gerard, informed of his affliction, hastened to visit him. He awakened his confidence in the Blessed Virgin, made the Sign of the Cross over him and left him. At the same moment the pain ceased, never to return.

In 1753, a fearful epidemic ravaged the city of Lacedonia. The victims were numberless, and the whole city was in mourning. The Bishop sent for Gerard, and the thaumaturgus was received as an Angel from Heaven. On beholding the joy of the inhabitants, one would have said that the scourge had already disappeared. The entrance of the servant of God into the desolate city resembled the passage of the Saviour through the cities and towns of Judea. Canon Saponiero was the first to experience the salutary influence of his presence. He was almost dying when Gerard went to visit him: "Reverend Father," said Gerard, "give glory to God, for you are cured." At the same time he made on his forehead the Sign of the Cross, which restored him to perfect health. He likewise cured the canon's brother, who was lying in extremity. "Blessed be God!" exclaimed the sick man on seeing Gerard enter. "Rejoice," responded the Saint, "your fever is gone." The sickness had indeed disappeared. All the sick of Lacedonia begged the favor of a visit from him. He was seen traversing the city, distributing to all the consolations of his charity without distinction of persons. Some he exhorted to patience, others he disposed for death, and a great number he cured. One would have said that a celestial power radiated from him for the cure of body and soul.

One day, Gerard was seriously ill and confined to bed at the house of the archpriest Don Salvadore at Oliveto. Brother Francesco Fiore had come to meet him there, but he too was seized with such an attack of fever that he had to be put to bed as quickly as possible on the ground floor. When Gerard heard of it, he said to the archpriest and his brother, who was a physician: "Be so kind as to say to Brother Francesco that he must in obedience shake off the fever, get up and come to me, for with the business I have at hand, I cannot spend my time taking care of a sick man." The doctor smiled, but Gerard went on: "Be so kind, if you please, as to do what I ask." At the order from Gerard, Brother Francesco was suddenly restored, and he went immediately to join his holy companion. As the doctor was wondering at so prompt a cure, the servant of God said to him: "Be not astonished. It is the effect of holy obedience." It was at this same period that he cured the archpriest's sister, who also had been attacked by a deadly fever. Hardly had he uttered the words: "See, you are cured," than the fever ceased.

Bartolomeo Melchiore of Bissaccia, a young married man, had fallen into a sort of decline, which caused him to pass for stupid or possessed by the devil. His friends took him to Campagna to implore the intercession of St. Antonio, but without success. When Gerard saw him, he said: "It is nothing, my friend. Health will return." He recited some prayers over the patient's head. The latter was suddenly cured and began to chant with his liberator a canticle of thanksgiving.

Lella Cocchia, of whom we have already spoken, had several months previously become insane. She uttered a thousand horrible things. Gerard, by merely signing her with the Cross, restored her so perfectly that she began at once to chant the praises of the Blessed Virgin.

A lady of Calitri named Angela Rinaldi was suddenly seized with a violent headache at the house of the Berilli family. Seeing Gerard's hat in a corner of the room, she put it on her head, saying, "Let us see whether the brother is a Saint." Her pain instantly ceased.

The same Berilli family, noticing that Gerard's shoes were very much worn, had new ones made for him and preserved the old through devotion. One of the children was attacked by violent intestinal pains, and no remedy could relieve him. The thought came to him to apply the Saint's shoes, and thanks to the virtue of the relics, he was instantly cured. These shoes became celebrated in Calitri. They were constantly going the rounds from one sick person to another; a host of wonders recompensed their confidence.

Going one day into a house of Auletta, the good brother found a girl in horrible convulsions. Her parents begged him to bless her, which he did with the Sign of the Cross. The convulsions ceased instantly, and from that day the poor girl was entirely delivered from them, although very subject to them before.

A poor young man, afflicted with a cancer in the leg, had himself taken to Iliceto, that he might commend himself to the prayers of the humble Redemptorist. Gerard, full of compassion, uncovered the diseased leg, and beholding it frightfully eaten away by the cancer (oh, heroic mortification of the

Saints!), he knelt and applied his lips to cleanse the wounds. "Confidence, my brother," he said as he finished, "you will be cured!" Then he bandaged the leg with clean linen. At that instant, the pains ceased, and the next day the leg was found completely cured.

Gerard did not forget his dear city of Muro in the distribution of heavenly favors. A lady of that city named Vitromilla had in her service a young relative who had been given up by the physicians. Vitromilla was so distressed at their decision that Gerard's heart was moved. "Have confidence in God and be consoled," he said to her. "Go home, and make the Sign of the Cross three times on the forehead of the sick girl, and she will be cured." The lady did as she had been told, and the girl was cured instantly.

The son of Alessandro Piccolo of Muro had a severe fall. He lay on the ground without speech or motion. "He is dying! It is all over with him," resounded on all sides. The servant of God, touched by the affliction of Alessandro, his friend and host, approached the youth, made the Sign of the Cross on his forehead and said to him: "It is nothing, my son, it is nothing." At these words, the dying boy rose up perfectly well.

A workman of Muro went one day on a pilgrimage to the Virgin of Caposele to obtain the cure of his child, afflicted with scrofula. The brother, taking a little of his saliva, put it upon the throat of the child, promising that the evil would not reappear. The cure was perfect.

A priest of Muro named Donat Spicci, having gone to Caposele to make a retreat, asked Brother Gerard to give him a remedy for a blind relative of the archpriest. The holy brother gave him a vial of water. For eight days, the blind girl bathed her eyes with it and then saw perfectly.

We must not think that the servant of God cured indiscriminately all the sick who had recourse to him with confidence. Sometimes bodily infirmity is willed by God for the salvation and sanctification of the soul. Msgr. Muyo, Bishop of Muro, one day received a visit from Gerard. He was at the time suffering severely from gout in his hands and feet. "My dear Gerard," he said, "beg God to deliver me from my pains."

"Monsignore, suffer with patience," replied Gerard, "for it is not to the glory of God that you should be delivered."

He made the same reply to Judith Frederici. This girl had entirely lost her sight. Her mother came to beg the thaumaturgus to ask of God the cure of her dear child. "I will do it," said Gerard. But soon he returned to the mother and said: "If your daughter recovers her sight, it will be to her loss. Submit to the will of God. The child will, however, be indemnified, for she will have more talent than others."

9. HIS POWER OVER HEARTS

THE prophetic spirit hovered over Gerard's head. His glance penetrated the inmost conscience.

He commanded nature with the voice of a master. At his word the sick were instantaneously cured. All this was doubtless very wonderful, but there was in the servant of God something still more deserving of admiration, and that was his power over hearts. He, the humble lay brother, had the gift of converting sinners, of comforting souls and of directing them in the sublime ways of perfection. It is useless to dwell longer on this subject. The foregoing pages prove that Gerard had the gift of moving hearts at pleasure.

Msgr. Nicolai, Archbishop of Conza, came to pass some days at the convent of Caposele, accompanied by a secretary, who was not in Holy Orders. He was a genial man, of great business aptitude and consequently dear to the prelate. But alas, his conscience was in a deplorable state, and God revealed it to His servant! To gain the confidence of the stranger, the zealous Redemptorist made it a point to meet him everywhere, greeting him in a friendly way, replying to his jokes and laughing at his sallies of wit. One day, seeing him very well disposed toward him, Gerard called him aside into the oratory. There, throwing himself at the man's feet, he said with tears in his eyes: "My friend, I cannot understand how you can be so merry, living as you do in enmity with God."

The secretary, quite abashed, also fell on his knees and confessed everything, weeping and imploring the help of Gerard's counsel and prayers. The latter encouraged him to call on the infinite mercy of God and led him to make a firm and sincere resolution. The secretary, troubled by the unexpected revelation, went at once to find Father Fiocchi and related to him all that had passed between himself and Gerard. "It is either God or the devil who has revealed my life to him. But it cannot be the devil, since I am full of repentance." After his interview with Father Fiocchi, he made his Confession and renounced his moral disorders. When he went to the church to communicate, Gerard was there before him to remind him of a sin that he had forgotten.

The sudden change of the secretary was noticed by all. From a jester, he had become a grave and serious man. The Archbishop, who could not divine the cause, asked him whence had come such a metamorphosis. The secretary, bursting into tears, answered in the words of the Samaritan woman: "Come and see a man who has told me all things whatsoever I have done." He then disclosed to the Archbishop the sad state in which he had heretofore lived and how he had been delivered from it by the care of good Brother Gerard.

This change was not less astonishing to the Archbishop's circle. "There is some mystery here," said the Superior of the seminary to the newly converted secretary. "I no longer see in you that gaiety which accompanied you everywhere. What can be the cause of it?"

"What!" replied the secretary, "do you not know what happened to me at Caposele? My dear canon, I was living in sin, and Brother Gerard, without knowing me, made me see clearly the miserable state of my soul."

The man had so much compunction that he revealed his conduct to everyone, as well as the manner in which the charitable Redemptorist had converted him. The Archbishop, seeing his happy dispositions, hastened to send him to Rome, provided with letters of recommendation to Msgr. Casone, his near relative. The latter heard from the lips of the secretary the history of his conversion and thus acquired for Gerard one more admirer. Conversing one day with a Cardinal, the prelate informed him of what had happened to the secretary of the Archbishop of Conza. The Cardinal was so struck by it that he wanted to become acquainted with the holy brother and so wrote to the Archbishop to send him to Rome. But when the letter arrived, the friend of God had passed to a better life.

The humble brother won to Jesus Christ the owner of a foundry at Calabria, who lived at Rochetta. Once, when Gerard was passing through that locality, they spoke to him of this man, who was living in sin, to the great scandal of the public. Gerard sent for him and exposed to him his most secret sins. The humbled sinner entered into himself, melted into tears, hastened to be reconciled with God and ever after persevered in a good life.

A man of Lacedonia was dying, his conscience laden with crimes and no one could succeed in converting him. Gerard was asked to visit the hardened sinner. He went in all haste. On entering the sickroom, he threw himself on his knees and recited an *Ave Maria.* Instantly, the dying man humbled himself, repented and received the Last Sacraments with great devotion.

There was in the same city a rich man who had for many years lived far from God. His poor wife came in tears to supplicate Gerard to ask God for her husband's conversion. It did not take long for the servant of God to change the dispositions of that hardened heart.

To convert sinners, he had recourse sometimes to the most terrifying prodigies. A nobleman, who was making the exercises of a retreat, was resolved in his heart not to abandon a certain occasion of sin. Gerard knew of it by revelation. He hastened to call the sinner apart and to abjure him to break his accursed chains. Seeing his efforts to be useless, he turned to Our Lord and begged Him to show this rebellious heart the fire of Hell and the frightful torments awaiting him if he did not change his life. At the same instant, the chamber became a furnace filled with the flames of Hell. At the horrible spectacle, the gentleman cast himself trembling at the feet of the Saint, weeping, sighing and promising to reform. He kept his word.

Gerard knew how to console as well as to convert souls: A man of distinction came to make a retreat at Iliceto, but after the first sermons, he conceived so great a despair of salvation that he began to revolve in his mind the blackest thoughts. While in this state, Gerard entered his room. "What is the matter with you, my dear friend? Chase away that spirit of distrust. It comes from Hell, for God and the Blessed Virgin are obliged to help you." The man was abashed at seeing his thought discovered, but this trouble left him instantly.

A pious lady, having heard the brother's holiness very much praised, desired to submit to him some doubts of conscience that she had dared not disclose to anyone else. But when she found herself in his presence, she became so frightened that she could not open her lips. Gerard, beholding her embarrassment, said to her: "Listen to me, I will speak for you." Thereupon he made known to her all that had passed in her soul. The lady afterward declared that no one in the world knew what the man of God revealed to her, and that the visit had greatly consoled her.

A Benedictine religious of Calitri long endured a sort of agony from scruples. Without uttering one word, Gerard laid before her all her troubles and then gave her counsel so wise that soon her interior trials were changed into ineffable consolations.

Gerard had a special gift for drawing souls to Jesus Christ, the Divine Spouse. This was the exquisite gift of our seraphic Redemptorist, a gift which he owed, without doubt, to his virginal purity and his tender love for Jesus Christ. Many young persons, at the mere sight of this angel of innocence, resolved to give themselves entirely to God. He could discover by intuition whether a soul had a religious vocation. Then he would make it a duty to manifest it to her and help her by his advice. Sometimes he would furnish her the means of getting the necessary dowry, and he gave himself no rest until he had obtained her reception into a convent. How many maidens owe to him their entrance into the cloister! How many monasteries, thanks to his zeal, received excellent recruits! How often did he esteem it an honor to accompany the parents when they themselves went to offer their children to the Lord! How many miracles did he perform on such journeys!

Besides the number of young girls whom he introduced into these gardens of piety, he caused to be received in the convent of Foggia his own niece, the two daughters of Costantino Capucci, his friend, and twelve other young persons connected with that pious family.

He predicted to a young pupil at one of the convents that she would become a religious, would quit the convent, but would hasten to return in order to escape the dangers of the world. This religious, this same Gertrude Cecilia of whom we have already spoken, died in great fervor in 1830.

Vincenza Palmieri, of an opulent family of Naples, went to finish her education with the Dominican nuns of Corato. One day Gerard said to her: "You have now no taste for the religious life. You ardently look forward to returning to your family. But one day you will be a religious in this convent. You will live a long and edifying life." The prediction was realized. Vincenza became a very fervent Dominican and died at nearly a hundred years old.

When the holy brother was soliciting alms for the poor convent of Iliceto, the Cianci family were desirous of giving him hospitality. One day at the dinner hour he took by the hand a little girl of four or five years old, saying: "I want to sit near this child at table because she will one day be a religious." Indeed, she entered the Benedictine convent of Atella, where she led a holy life under the name of Sister Maria. In her old age she used to tell with pleasure of having once dined at the side of a Saint.

10. HIS POWER OVER HELL

A FRIEND of God such as Gerard could not fail to be in conflict with Hell. His zeal for the salvation of souls and the striking conversions that he made roused against him the rage of the demons. Those accursed spirits tried by every means to discourage him and thwart his pious undertakings. They frequently appeared to him, both by day and by night, threatening and maltreating him, to force him to cease robbing them of souls. His directors have declared that they went so far as to drag him along the corridors of the house. "You will not give up," said a demon to him one night. "Ah! I will take no rest till I have chased you out of this world."

Sometimes the wicked spirits fell upon him and held him down with such force that he ran the risk of being stifled. They loaded him with blows so violent that his whole body seemed to be one wound and his bones broken. One day when he was cooking, several demons tempted him to throw himself into the fire. Again, they used to appear to him under the form of furious dogs ready to tear him to pieces. "You may bark," said Gerard, "but as I have on my side Mary, my Mother, and Jesus Christ, my Saviour, you cannot bite me." These assaults took place especially on Friday nights.

In this savage struggle, the faithful servant of Christ always remained the victor, for he had immense empire over the demons. On a certain Sunday, two young men were seen standing immovable at one side of our church. No one knew who they were or whence they came. But as soon as Gerard perceived them, he went straight up to them, saying: "What are you doing there? This is not your place. In the name of God, return to Hell." The demons, for such they were, instantly disappeared. No one knew what they were after, but the fact is undeniable. Several of our brethren were witnesses of it.

Here is something still more surprising: Returning one day from Melfi to Iliceto, Gerard lost his way in the woods of Ofanto. The night was already advanced. A thick fog, lurid lightning, the crashing thunder, torrents rolling down their waters swollen by the rains, a thousand abysses yawning in the darkness, all conspired to render Gerard's position affrighted. Suddenly at the edge of a deep ravine rose up a human form. It dashed toward the servant of God, crying in a brutal tone: "The hour of vengeance has come!" Gerard understood that he was in the presence of the demon, but he was far from being frightened. "Abominable monster," he said, "in the name of the Most Holy Trinity, I command you to take my horse by the bridle and lead me to Lacedonia without doing me any injury." At this order, the demon, murmuring, bowed his head and, taking the bridle, quietly conducted horse and rider to Lacedonia.

Constantino Capucci, who on that same evening gave hospitality to the good brother, thus relates the fact. "About six o'clock one evening, I heard a rap at the door, and on asking who was there, I was very much surprised to hear Brother Gerard's voice. I opened quickly, and seeing him all wet, I said, 'O my dear brother, what, is it you! But at what an hour, and in what weather!'

'My dear Constantino,' he replied with his usual frankness, 'may the will of God be done! I was returning from Melfi, but the darkness, the fog and the rain came upon me. I lost my way. I was in the midst of such precipices on the banks of the Ofanto that, if God had not come to my aid, I should have lost my life. While on the edge of an abyss, some one suddenly came toward me.

"This is where I want you," he said. "Now I am your master . . ."

At first, I was a little frightened, but instantly commending myself to Our Lord, I saw that I had to deal with the demon. "Vile beast," I said to him, "I command you, in the name of the Most Holy Trinity, to take the bridle of my horse and lead me straight to Lacedonia without doing me any harm." And thus, guided by the demon, I was saved from danger. Were it not for him, I should not be alive; I should be buried in the ravines of Ofanto. When I reached the church of the Most Holy Trinity, the enemy of God said to me: "Here you are at Lacedonia," and disappeared.'" Gerard himself related this incident to Fathers Fiocchi and Juvenal.

A similar adventure occurred to him on the road from Castelgrande: He had had to climb a steep mountain, and he was exhausted from fatigue. Suddenly a white horse presented itself before him, and the man of God mounted it. But soon the animal left the good road and turned into one bordered by precipices and ending in an abyss. Without special assistance, the holy Redemptorist would have perished. But confiding in God, he ordered the horse to return to the good road, and it obeyed.

At the voice of Gerard, Hell was forced sometimes to intervene even for the salvation of souls. A man of Castelgrande named Francesco Mugnone had come to make a retreat at Caposele. Meeting him, Gerard said to him: "Francesco, have you made a good Confession?"

"Yes," answered the other.

"No, it was not well made. Look what you have behind you."

Francesco, turning, saw at his side the demon under a horrible shape. Filled with fright, he went quickly to repeat his Confession.

Another sinner attended a retreat merely through

human respect. Resolved not to be converted, he concealed his sins from the confessor. He was in the choir assisting at Mass and getting ready to approach the Holy Table. Suddenly, Gerard approached and made him a sign to follow him. He took him into a room and there, after laying before him the enormity of sacrilege, he caused two demons to appear, who under the form of bears, threatened to strangle him. Overwhelmed with fear, the man was converted and entirely changed his life.

How many possessed owed their deliverance to this great enemy of Hell! One day when at Oliveto, he saw a crowd around a demoniac who, writhing with rage, suffered no one to approach him. But Gerard went straight up to him and asked him who he was.

"I am the devil," answered the possessed, "I am the devil!"

"In the name of the Most Holy Trinity, I command you to quit this creature," said the brother.

"I am going," replied the demon, "but you will pay for it!"

The cincture of the angelic brother possessed a special power for driving away impure spirits. Called one day to the assistance of a possessed person, it sufficed for him to put his cincture around the man in order to make the demon take to hasty flight.

One day when praying in the church of Castelgrande, he heard a great tumult. It was caused by two possessed persons who, on seeing him, cried out in rage: "Who is this man that persecutes us everywhere?" Soon after, the servant of God saw at his feet two mothers supplicating him to deliver their two daughters, long possessed by the devil. Touched with compassion, Gerard gave them his cincture. "Go home," he said to them, "and put this cincture on the poor girls, and they will be delivered. But after that, they must go to Confession and Communion at once. The devils will then return no more." The mothers obeyed, and their daughters were delivered from the power of the devil.

Another fact of this kind took place in the same church: Gerard was praying before the Blessed Sacrament when suddenly he heard a noise. Going to discover the cause, he found a young girl lying extended, face downward, on the ground. She was possessed, and she had the habit, above all during the Holy Sacrifice, of vomiting horrible blasphemies against the Most Blessed Sacrament and the Blessed Virgin. She was even possessed by an impure spirit. The charitable brother, after having raised his eyes to Heaven and having addressed a short prayer to Our Lord, bade the unclean spirit cease his evil work. Instantly, the poor girl was freed. Thenceforth, to the great admiration of the whole locality, she was seen practicing the exercises of a devout life.

The damned themselves were subservient to the orders of Blessed Gerard for the conversion of souls. In a retreat preached at Iliceto, an unfortunate man was about to approach the Holy Table in the state of sin. The good religious at once went to him. "My brother," he said, "here is a sin that you have not confessed. Perhaps you do not know that a sacrile-gious Communion is a great misfortune. If you are ignorant of it, behold the horrible appearance of a sacrilegious soul!" He had scarcely uttered the words when a lost soul appeared. The frightful sight so ter-rified the sinner that he was instantly converted.

—Part Five—

DEATH AND GLORIFICATION
OF ST. GERARD

1. HIS LAST ILLNESS

THE year 1755 was a painful but glorious one for our Saint. He spent the month of July at San Gregorio, continuing his collection of alms for the building of the convent at Caposele. He was suddenly seized with a hemorrhage and burning fever. The physician ordered him to Oliveto, where the milder air would be better for his present state. There, the hemorrhages, far from decreasing, were very seriously increased. Seeing himself reduced to such a state, the obedient religious wrote to his Rector, Father Cajone: "If you wish me to return to the convent I shall do so immediately. If you wish me to continue the collection, I shall continue it. Send me a strong obedience, and all will go well. I am grieved to have to give you this anxiety, but do not be alarmed, it is nothing. Commend me to God, that I may in all things do His holy will." The Superior was afflicted at this news, but he judged it well to confide the invalid to the charity of the archpriest Don Salvadore until he should be in a state to travel.

At the end of eight days Gerard, feeling that he was growing worse, thought it time to return to his convent. He arrived on the 31st of August in such a state of exhaustion that he appeared no longer a man. "At first sight of him," wrote Father Cajone, "I had to do violence to myself to keep back the tears." His confreres marveled at his joy and the unalterable serenity of his soul in the midst of sufferings so great. The fever, far from leaving him on his return, daily increased, and soon it was accompanied by the most alarming symptoms. Dysentery reduced him to extreme weakness, and he was covered with profuse perspiration. Delirium and fainting spells were almost continual. The demon, beholding him reduced to this extremity, appeared to him, offering him health and life. "Begone, villainous beast!" replied the heroic religious. "I will but what God wills, and I order you not to molest me."

The Father Rector asked him whether he had conformed in everything to the will of God, to which the good brother answered: "I look upon my bed as the will of God for me and consider that there I am nailed to the divine will. It seems to me that the will of God and I have become one and the same thing." Later on, he caused to be placarded on the door of his cell in large characters: "Here we do the will of God, as God wills it and as long as God wills it."

His hemorrhages increased from day to day. In four days he lost several quarts of blood. Dr. Santorelli asked him whether he desired to live or die. "Neither to live nor to die," answered Gerard. "I want only what God wills. I would indeed wish to die and be united to Him, but I am afflicted at the thought of death because I have suffered nothing for Jesus Christ."

On re-entering his poor cell, he had had a large crucifix covered with wounds and blood placed opposite his bed, and at it he never ceased to gaze lovingly. Weak as he was, he knelt before it one or two hours every day to unite his sufferings with those of the Divine Redeemer. His ordinary prayer was: "I suffer, O my God, from having nothing to suffer. To suffer, my well-beloved Jesus, and not to die!" Father Cajone, entering his chamber one day, found him as if in agony. But the pious Redemptorist cast his eyes suddenly on the crucifix, his features became animated, and a rosy flush colored his cheeks. "Ah, Father!" he said, sighing ardently, "ah, Father, great is my desire to unite myself to my God!"

When his illness became known, crowds of priests and laymen flocked to visit him, still desiring to receive from his lips some salutary advice. Overcome by his unalterable conformity to the will of God, they went away, saying: "Behold how the Saints speak and die!" Although on the brink of the tomb, the zealous brother still wanted to write some letters in order to console and to fortify in the Christian virtues the souls whom his counsels had directed.

His illness increasing, it was thought well to administer to him the Holy Viaticum. During the ceremony, Gerard lay on his bed in an attitude so respectful that the mere sight of him inspired piety and devotion. Father Buonamano, holding the Sacred Host in his hand, addressed to Gerard these words: "Behold the Lord, who is your Father, and who in a little while will be your Judge. Re-animate your faith and make the preparatory acts." The dying Saint responded with confidence and humility: "Thou knowest, O my God, that all I have done, all that I have said has been for Thy glory. I die content, because I hope I have never sought but Thy will." After communicating, he wished to remain alone for a while in prayer and to pour out the affections of his heart into the Heart of Jesus.

The servant of God received during his illness a visit from a young man who, by his libertinism, had plunged several families into grief. Gerard had no knowledge by natural means of the youth's misconduct. But, enlightened by the Spirit that sounds the depths of consciences, he said to him as soon as he laid his eyes on him: "How have you the audacity to present yourself here, you who make so many tears flow? And now you want Jesus Christ to grant you pardon!" It is to be hoped that these words withdrew the unfortunate man from his downward career.

On the 6th of September, the sick brother becoming constantly weaker, they were about to administer to him Extreme Unction when there arrived a letter addressed to him from Father Fiocchi, his director. It commanded him to cease raising blood and to get well. The Superior was absent at the time. After reading the letter, Gerard placed it respectfully on his heart. Just at this moment, Dr. Santorelli entered and, finding his patient very recollected, took the letter in his hand, asking what it was. The holy brother answered: "It is the obedience that Father Fiocchi has sent me. He wishes me to stop spitting blood."

"Well," replied the doctor, "what do you think you'll do?" For his only answer, Gerard said to the infirmarian: "Take the basin away." From that moment the hemorrhages ceased, but the dysentery continued. "Of what avail to cease spitting blood," said the doctor to him, "if you allow the other evil to continue?"

"I have received no obedience for that," answered Gerard. The doctor hurried after Father Garzilli to ask him to come and make Gerard understand that obedience wished him to be perfectly, and not partly cured. The Father went immediately to the sickroom. "Do you not scruple to obey in this way?" he asked. "Father Fiocchi commands you not only to stop spitting blood, but also to shake off the fever and to rise in good health." Gerard humbly replied: "If it is so, Father, I am going to obey in every point."

When the doctor presented himself in the afternoon, Gerard said to him: "Tomorrow I shall get up." And seeing him smile, he repeated: "Yes, tomorrow I shall get up, and if you wish, I shall even eat something." The doctor, noticing his tone of confidence, resolved to put him to the test. Just at that moment there came to the sick man a little basket of peaches. "If you promise to execute the obedience of Father Fiocchi," he said, "I will permit you to eat one."

"May the obedience be fulfilled, and may God be glorified!" replied Gerard. As soon as he had eaten one, they gave him a second and then a third.

Next morning, Dr. Santorelli went straight to Gerard's room and, not finding him there, asked what had become of him. He was told that he was walking in the garden. "O power of holy obedience!" exclaimed this man of faith, "what prodigies dost thou not bring about!" He hastened to the garden, where he was met by the brother, who said to him: "Doctor, I would have been dead today if God had not willed to manifest how much He loves obedience. Know, however, that it is of this sickness and in this year that I shall die." Great was the joy of the community when they beheld Gerard taking his place in the refectory. A carpenter of Muro named Filippo Galella was at that time doing some work in the convent. "My dear fellow townsman," said Gerard to him, "I was about to die on the 8th of September, but Our Lord has prolonged my life for some days."

2. HIS LAST MOMENTS

GERARD, the Saint of Obedience, obeying even as his Divine Master, unto death, was indeed restored, but not for long. Seeing his brethren rejoicing over his cure, he said to them: "It is to manifest His glory and to show what obedience can do that God has thus acted in my regard. But I am going to die. In a few days I shall be in eternity." On October 5th the fever returned, as well as the dysentery and the hemorrhages. On the evening before, he had said to his friend Dr. Santorelli, "Doctor, the other day, I fulfilled the obedience, but remember what I told you, that I shall die soon. The time has come. I am attacked by a sickness that has no remedy." He returned to bed and thought no longer of anything but of preparing for death.

The lover of Jesus Crucified had had all his life an ardent thirst to share in the sufferings of the Passion of Jesus Christ. Feeling his end approaching, he asked God for the favor of experiencing both the interior and the exterior pains that Jesus suffered in His agony. Although careful to conceal his sufferings, he could not prevent his attendants from perceiving something of them. One day when he was entertaining himself alone with his crucifix, he exclaimed: "Lord, help me in this purgatory!" The doctor, entering at the moment, heard the words and asked what they meant. "Dear doctor," answered the dying man, "I earnestly asked Jesus Christ for the grace to pay my debts in this world by suffering for love of Him, and He has heard me. I am enduring a true purgatory, but I console myself with the thought that I am giving pleasure to Jesus Christ." Another day, he again said to the doctor: "I am enduring a martyrdom. I have no longer strength to speak."

A priest named Gerardo Gisone, who afterward entered the Congregation of Redemptorists, came to consult Gerard on the affairs of his conscience. The holy brother, even before hearing a word from his lips, revealed to him the state of his soul and gave him wise advice. Then he said to him: "Pray for me, for I am suffering intensely."

"What are you suffering?"

"I am in the Wounds of Jesus Christ, and His Wounds are in me. I am undergoing all the pains, all the sufferings that Jesus Christ endured in His Passion."

His state of suffering, far from afflicting him, consoled him very much. Of one thing only did he complain, and that was of being so great a burden on the community. The doctor, having prescribed a certain remedy, ordered that a brother should sit up with him in order to administer a dose toward midnight. "O doctor," exclaimed the charitable religious, "that will only make me suffer!" And he repeated the words with signs of lively trouble. Prayers offered in common for his cure also gave him pain. "I am only a useless creature," he would say. "I do not deserve all that." Reflecting on the expense occasioned by his medicines, he would sorrowfully say: "Of what use have I ever been to the community that it should undergo so much expense for me?"

Brother Stefano Sperduto asked him one day whether he had any disquietude. "I have done everything for the love of God," answered Gerard. "I have had Him in view in all things. I have always kept myself in His presence, and as I have desired only His divine will, I die happy."

His holy indifference with regard to remedies of all kinds and his perfect obedience to the doctor and the infirmarian never flagged. When they offered him some bitter drink, he took it instantly, despite the natural repugnance it excited and which caused him frequent vomiting. Sometimes he was heard to cry out: "My God, I have not the strength for it!" But at the sound of the word "obedience," he took all that they offered him.

And now occurred a prodigy which testified to the holiness of the dying brother. A delicious and truly heavenly odor, which could be compared to nothing earthly, filled the infirmary. This phenomenon was so much the more astonishing as it was in so great contrast with the character of the disease and the constant exudations from the body of the invalid.

Doubtless, God willed to attest by this marvel the perfect purity of His servant. And indeed, this was not the first time that the sweet odor was noticed. The brother who nursed him said one day: "Brother Gerard, you have some perfume about you in spite of the prohibition of the Rule."

"Not at all," replied the Saint. However, as the fragrance became more and more perceptible, the infirmarian thought it his duty to mention it to the Father Rector. The latter excused the invalid, saying that God had shown him great favor, and then said no more. The brother did not fail to notice that the perfume proceeded from the expectorations of the Saint. Before, at Oliveto, Gerard's chamber was redolent with the perfume of Paradise, so that, as Giuseppe Salvadore testified, when the people of Oliveto came to speak to the holy man, the sweet odor guided them to his room.

On October 13th, Gerard received a visit from the physician, Don Salvadore of Oliveto, who was accompanied by the Reverend Prosper de Aquila and a young villager. The last named, in his timidity, dared not enter the room. But the friend of God called him, pointed to the harpsichord, which happened to be there, and begged him to play something. Great was the embarrassment of the rustic at this request, and the visitors could not suppress a laugh. The Saint insisted. Urged by those around, the young man, who was ignorant of even the first elements of the musical art, sat down at the instrument, laid his heavy hands on the keyboard and drew forth the most melodious sounds. He afterward declared that, while touching the keys, his fingers had obeyed an irresistible impulse.

Brother Gerard received Communion every morning. On the 15th of October, the feast of St. Teresa, he said to Dr. Santorelli: "Dear doctor, commend me to St. Teresa and offer Holy Communion for my intention." He himself received Communion on that day with ravishing piety. "It is an Angel," said the assistants with emotion. "It is a Seraph who is uniting himself with the Divine Essence." As a proof of his lively faith and ardent love, he asked for the corporal on which the Sacred Host had reposed, placed it on his heart and kept it there till his last sigh.

On this day there was heard in the chamber of the dying Seraph a concert so ravishing that Father Petrella, who was present, thought himself in Paradise. It was the heavenly Angels who had come to summon an earthly angel to the nuptials of the Lamb. Gerard then predicted the exact hour of his death. "Today, the feast of St. Teresa," he said, "is a recreation day of the Rule for the community. Tomorrow, it will again be recreation. Why? Because I shall die tonight."

In the evening, he asked the hour. "Six o'clock," was the answer. "I have still six hours to live," he remarked, and then said to the infirmarian: "My dear brother, tonight, at such an hour, I must die. Clothe me, for I want to recite the Office of the Dead for my soul."

As the doctor was about to retire, Gerard, contrary to his custom, foreseeing his approaching death, asked him to stay with him. But Doctor Santorelli, finding him a little better, excused himself, saying that he had other sick to visit. The next day the doctor understood that the holy brother, his intimate friend, wished to have him present at his last sigh.

Toward seven o'clock, a messenger arrived from Oliveto with a letter addressed to Brother Gerard. It was from the archpriest, who wrote to beg him to commend to God an affair connected with his parish. He had commenced a sanctuary to the Mother of God, and a large limestone cupola was threatening to collapse. The holy religious, to whom God had revealed the contents of the letter, said to the messenger as soon as he saw him: "Let them go on with the building. The cupola will suffer no damage." Then, giving the messenger a little dust from the tomb of St. Teresa, he directed it to be scattered over the cupola. His prediction was literally accomplished.

Human words cannot express with what presence of mind and humility he prepared to appear before his Judge. Although he had preserved his baptismal innocence, he was heard reciting the *Miserere*, seated on his bed, with devotion so great that it drew tears from all who approached him.

About eight o'clock, he several times repeated: "My God, where art Thou? Show me Thy face!" And turning to the assistants, he said to them: "Help me to unite myself to God." They asked him whether he had anything on his conscience. "Why do you speak to me of inquietude?" he answered quickly.

Between ten and eleven, he became agitated and cried out: "What are those two miserable wretches doing there? Quick, put them out of the door!" Without doubt, they were demons. Regaining his serenity, he said joyously: "Ah, see the Madonna! Let us kneel down." And kneeling on his couch, he appeared absorbed in deep ecstasy.

As the night was already advanced, and no one imagined he would die so soon, the community retired, with the exception of one brother who was to remain as nurse. A little before his death, Gerard asked for a drink, and the infirmarian ran to get some water. On his return, he found the dying brother leaning against the wall, and he thought him asleep. But soon he perceived that his agony had begun, and he hastened to arouse Father Buonamano. The latter hurried to the sick room, and while he was pronouncing the words of absolution, the beautiful soul of Gerard soared to God, freed from its earthly wrapping less by the force of sickness than by the ardor of divine love, as many witnesses deposed. This fact was also stated by the postulator of the Cause of Beatification: *"Potius amore, quam morbo consumptus, uti deponunt omnes fere testes, animam Deo reddidit."*

3. HIS FUNERAL OBSEQUIES

SO died our Seraph on the night of October 15-16, 1755, toward midnight. He was twenty-nine years and six months old. As soon as he expired, his body exhaled a most agreeable odor, which pervaded the whole convent. At that same hour he appeared, clothed in his religious soutane, to a pious soul who was very devoted to him; and a little after, he appeared a second time, richly arrayed and resplendent with glory. "Oh!" said he to her, "how generously God rewards the little pains that we suffer for Him on earth!" He appeared also at the same hour to Father Petrella and showed to him a ray of the glory with which he was crowned in Heaven.

Father Buonamano, who was acting Superior, ordered at once a discipline in common to thank

God for having granted to a member of the Congregation so holy a death. One would have said that all saw the holy Redemptorist in heavenly glory. In the midst of these transports, one brother hurried to ring the bell, as on great solemnities. When reproved for so doing, he declared that he had acted under an impulse that could not be resisted.

Toward three in the morning, Father Buonamano, urged by an inspiration from above, had the holy body bled. "Brother Gerard," he said, "during your life you were always obedient. I command you in the name of the Most Holy Trinity to give us a proof of your sanctity." They opened a vein in the right arm, and there immediately flowed forth more than two quarts of red blood. This prodigy crowned the general joy. They proceeded to steep linen in the blood, which they afterward distributed to the friends of the servant of God.

The news of this holy death was no sooner made known than crowds ran from all directions: poor and rich, priests and laymen, secular and regular, all wished to venerate the remains of him whom they called the Saint. One related a prophecy verified in his own person; another told how his interior had been read by Gerard; a third declared that he had been brought back to a good life by the brother. The poor, above all, the poor whom the charitable servant of God cherished so greatly, repeated with tears: "We have lost our father!" Not content with exalting his holiness, they began to take clippings from his hair and clothing, so that it was found necessary to place guards around the precious remains.

A lady of Caposele, Rosa Sturchio, who had always entertained profound veneration for Gerard, cast herself on her knees weeping before his remains, begging him to leave her a relic as a souvenir and sign of his protection. Suddenly, O prodigy, the Saint opened his mouth and let fall a tooth! The lady received it as a treasure, and it brought about two great miracles in her family. The first was the instantaneous return to health of her daughter, who was already in her agony, and the second was the happy delivery of her niece at the moment in which death seemed inevitable.

The funeral observances were performed in the presence of thousands from all parts. Father Garzilli sang the Mass, and Father Buonamano delivered a discourse so touching as to draw tears from his hearers.

Before burying the holy remains, the Father Minister ordered a second bleeding, commanding Gerard, as on the first occasion, to give up some blood. As before, it flowed abundantly. The members of the body were flexible, and a sweat so abundant flowed from the forehead that it could be gathered on handkerchiefs. The coffin was deposited in a special place before the sacristy.

The artist not having arrived in time to make a portrait of the servant of God, they had to be satisfied with a waxen cast. Later, the attempt was made to make his picture from this cast. As they could not succeed, Father Cajone, returning to the house, thus addressed the holy brother: "My dear Gerard, the painter cannot come to make your portrait. Show him how to accomplish it where he is." After this, the artist succeeded wonderfully. It seemed to him, he said, that some one was helping him to wield the brush. The portrait represents the holy Redemptorist in the position in which the archpriest Don Salvadore beheld him in ecstasy at Oliveto, holding the crucifix in one hand, with the other resting on his breast.

4. HIS MIRACLES

"THE remembrance of the wicked shall perish with them, but the memory of the just shall remain forever," says the Lord. Scarcely had the faithful servant of Jesus Christ expired when it pleased Heaven to give proofs of the immortal glory he was enjoying.

A. Prodigies in Favor of His Brethren

HIS brethren were the first to receive his favors. Father Cajone, being in great perplexity of mind and not knowing how to free himself, confidently resorted to Gerard. The latter delayed not to console him. He appeared to him all resplendent with the riches of glory and said: "Be at peace. All is over." The priest instantly recovered his interior peace and joy.

Brother Nicolo di Sapio, likewise, was plunged in the deepest affliction. He opened his heart to Father

Cajone, who advised him to have recourse to Brother Gerard. Nicolo's prayer was immediately heard.

Some one came one day to entreat Father Petrella earnestly to pray for the conversion of a poor sinner of Caposele. The Father replied: "I shall give an obedience to Brother Gerard to go hunt him up and make him enter into himself." Next day, the man came running in fright to the church, saying that Brother Gerard had appeared to him and remonstrated with him severely. He confessed with signs of lively repentance.

Father Tannoia was very ill. When about to breathe his last, he made a vow to write the Life of Brother Gerard, if he should be cured. We owe, therefore, his first biography to a miracle wrought by the Saint.

In 1846, our good brother suddenly cured Father Balducci, who had been attacked by very serious pulmonary trouble.

Father Saggese, who died in 1852, Archbishop of Chieri, had the tenderest devotion to the holy brother, for which he was magnificently recompensed. In his last illness, he had placed a relic of the Saint just opposite his bed. On more than one occasion, it was seen to emit rays of light which rested on the face of the dying man. The good prelate, inundated with consolation, a smile on his lips, never ceased repeating: "Blessed be the Lord! Blessed be the Lord!"

In 1858, in the convent of Wittem, Holland, one of our young students of philosophy suffered from constant nervous twitchings that never left him, day or night. For six months he took no nourishment.

The malady would soon have ended fatally, had not his confreres made for the dear invalid a novena to Brother Gerard. At the end of it, at the very moment that he received Holy Communion, the young religious felt himself cured. He arose and went to the church to thank his benefactor. That same day, he was able to make a long journey on foot. "Without this favor from our holy brother," he wrote thirty-five years after, "I should now be, as to my soul, either in Purgatory or in Heaven, as to the body, in the dear vault of Wittem. Happy fate, without doubt! But never would I have celebrated Holy Mass, never would I have poured out upon poor sinners—my well-beloved in Jesus and Mary—the Blood of Jesus to give them pardon and the treasures of Sanctifying Grace."

In 1860 our Brother, Conrad Stuifmeel, of the same convent of Wittem, was reduced to a state of complete prostration in consequence of continuous and copious hemorrhages. He made a novena to Brother Gerard. On the fifth day of the novena, he saw in a dream the great servant of God, who filled him with ineffable consolations and gave him perfect health. He was able to resume at once his hard labor.

B. Prodigies in Favor of His Friends

GERARD never forgot his friends before God. Dominico Camillo was united with him in the ties of friendship. On leaving Gerard one day, he exclaimed: "Would that I could have you always with me!"

"When you want me," responded Gerard, "call me, and I will come."

Several years after the Saint's death, Dominico went to the fair with a wagon laden with merchandise, which on the road sank so deep in the mud that it was impossible to get it out. Camillo recalled the promise made him. "Brother Gerard," he cried, "now's the time to keep your word. If you do not get me out of this fix, I'll never be able to go on!" Hardly had he spoken when the mules drew the wagon out of the rut with astonishing ease.

Donna Isabella Salvadore, niece of the good archpriest of Oliveto of whom we have made mention, was stricken with a serious illness that took her to within a hair's breadth of the tomb. In her extremity, she applied a piece of linen that had been saturated with the blood of the saintly brother; she was instantaneously cured. She procured the same favor for Cecilia de Binso, her friend, who was suffering from constant fevers.

Joseph Santorelli, like his grandfather, a physician, was seriously attacked by typhoid fever. His death appeared so certain that his relatives had already prepared the coffin and tapers for the funeral. His brother laid on his head the picture of Brother Gerard, the great friend of the family. Suddenly, to the amazement of those present, the sick man sat up in bed quite cured. The holy brother had appeared to him with the words: "Rise without fear."

In July, 1789, Dominico Bozzio of Caposele, attacked by a malignant fever, was given up by the physicians. The affliction of his family was very great, for he was leaving wife and children. His uncle, the Canon Bozzio, seeing him in this sad state, told him that Gerard had promised to take special care of his family when he should be in Heaven. "If that is so," said the sick man, "recall to him his promise." At once the whole family united in invoking with confidence the protection of the servant of God. One night Gerard appeared to the sick man and said to him with a joyous air, "We have settled everything." Dominico rose next morning perfectly cured.

Another gentleman of the same family of Bozzio of Caposele fell seriously ill. Dr. Santorelli gave him a relic of Gerard, telling him to commend himself to the good religious. Hardly had the sick man taken it into his hand when he fell asleep. On awakening, he exclaimed: "I have just seen Brother Gerard clothed as a missionary. He said to me, 'Love thy God who restores thee to health. Thou wilt have no more fever.'" In fact, to the great joy of his family, the sick man arose at once as if he had never been in other than perfect health.

C. Prodigies in Favor of Priests and Souls Consecrated to God

IN his numerous journeys, the humble brother had met only kindness among the clergy and religious. He wished, therefore, after his death to give them a large share in his influence with God.

A canon of Trevico named Ignazio Cozzo had for a long time suffered from a very painful rupture. One day he applied to it a piece of the clothing of the holy brother, saying: "My dear Gerard, if it can contribute to the glory of God and the good of my soul, deign to cure me." Instantly the trouble disappeared, never to return.

In 1787, a Benedictine religious of the convent of Sciacca, Sicily, had on her arm an incurable sore which caused her horrible suffering. Having received a picture of the Saint, she commended herself to him with the most lively confidence. When the surgeon came to dress the arm, he found it entirely cured.

Lorenzo Giliberti, Superior of the Seminary of Conza, suffered horrible pains from some internal trouble. The most skillful physicians had been consulted in vain. "It is all over with me," he said to a friend who was visiting him.

"Not at all," replied the visitor; "commend yourself to Brother Gerard. Carry his picture about you, and he will cure you." The Superior followed the advice and was instantly cured. The trouble never reappeared.

In 1840, Rafaelle Pitasse, a pupil of the monastery of Foggia, was instantly delivered from very serious eye trouble by using a letter of the Saint.

In 1840, a young man aspiring to the priesthood fell gravely ill. His hemorrhages were so frequent that the physician gave up all hopes of saving him.

As he had a sister in the convent of Ripacandida, the nuns were interested in him, and so they determined to send him a relic of Brother Gerard, whose memory was held in great veneration in their convent. They had a bone of the Saint. When they attempted to break it, in order to send the sick man a particle, it became soft as wax. To this first prodigy was joined a second. Hardly had they recited the *Gloria Patri* for the sick man nine times before the precious relic when they heard a number of sharp, successive blows, like, as one of the Sisters related, the blows of stones hurled by children against the church windows. By this sign the servant of God wished to indicate that the grace had been granted. The event confirmed the prediction, for at that same hour the invalid was cured. He continued to have excellent health and entered the priesthood.

In 1842, Mgr. Pasquale de Seriis, Protonotary Apostolic, who for eight days had suffered intolerable pains in the stomach, was suddenly cured by invoking the servant of God. Thenceforth, his health was most satisfactory.

On October 3, 1842, a priest named Raffaello Letitia lost in the great city of Naples a portfolio containing papers of the highest importance. He hastened to take the usual steps for recovering it, but all in vain. On the evening of the 4th he exclaimed: "Brother Gerard, you do so many favors for others. Grant me one also. Find my portfolio." Next morning, when he went to the post office to get a letter that he was expecting from Rome, an employee said to him: "Who sent you here? Is it not you who lost a portfolio? If you want it, ask it of such and such a person, who will give it to you." It is needless to describe the priest's joy.

In 1846, the archpriest of Palombara, Raffaello Spinelli, was reduced to extremity by pulmonary consumption. He had great devotion to our Saint. On awakening one morning, he asked who had entered his chamber. "No one," was the answer. The following morning, someone again entered; the visitor said to him: "I came yesterday morning and asked you what you wanted, but you did not answer me. Now, tell me very simply what you want."

"First, health of soul," responded the priest, "then that of the body." This said, he turned on the other side to see who had spoken to him. He beheld a tall person, his head uncovered, who on turning to go, held within his reach a chaplet. The priest, now thoroughly roused, asked whether his secretary had entered the room, but he was told that he had not. Now, the nocturnal visitor was none other than Brother Gerard, who had come to restore his health.

In 1859, a signal favor was granted to M. Jacques, the Director of the College of Waremme. "One winter morning," he himself relates, "the phosphorus from a burning match came in contact with a cut that I had on my right forefinger. In a few moments the swelling and pain were such that I already foresaw the necessity of a serious operation. I fell on my knees. A simple invocation to Brother Gerard effected a complete and instantaneous cure, so that even the old wound had disappeared. Some minutes after, I was able to celebrate the Holy Sacrifice."

In 1874, a Poor Clare, Sister Maria Teresa Bottiglieri, given up by the doctors and having received the Last Sacraments, recovered her health by invoking the Saint.

In 1875, a Poor Clare of Coregliano, Sister Maria Nazarina Via, was at the point of death in consequence of frequent hemorrhages. She laid on her breast a picture of Brother Gerard, saying: "If it is the will of God, deign to cure me perfectly." Hardly had she uttered the words when her sickness disappeared.

A priest of the diocese of Brooklyn in the United States became paralyzed in his hands. He could not use them. In 1881, after reading the life of the Saint, he felt inspired to make a novena to him for his cure. The novena was not ended before he was perfectly cured. As a mark of his gratitude, he sent twenty-five dollars toward defraying the expenses of his benefactor's Beatification.

D. PRODIGIES ON BEHALF OF THE SICK

GOD gives to certain Saints the power to cure one or other particular malady, but He seems to act with more liberality toward our Saint. Innumerable facts attest this.

In 1776, Lady Antonietta de Vallo fell desperately ill. A priest, a relative of hers, put under her pillow a relic of the holy religious and begged him to cure her. One night, Gerard appeared to the lady, made over her the Sign of the Cross and said to her: "Behold, you are cured!" As she did not know to whom she should attribute the favor, her friends showed her several pictures of the Saints. As soon as she saw that of Brother Gerard, "There," she exclaimed, "that is the one who cured me!"

The noble lady Maria Giordano of Corbara never ceased recommending herself to the servant of God. One day, when praying in our church of Caposele, Gerard appeared to her and said: "Prepare for great tribulations, but have courage. God will assist you." The prophecy was not long in being verified. The lady had much to suffer, but Gerard appeared to her again to sustain her in her severe trials.

Victorina Coccione fell from the top of a ladder and so injured one leg that she could not move in her bed without spasms of pain. A relative sent her a relic of the Saint. She applied it and was instantly cured.

In 1780, Leonarde Miocore was suddenly cured of eye trouble which had rendered her almost blind. Seeing the oculist shortly after, she said to him joyously: "You could not cure me, but I have just been consulting a doctor who knew how to do it."

"You are jesting," said the other.

"Look," she said, showing him her eyes. The physician examined them and declared them perfectly cured. "Here is my doctor," she said, holding up Brother Gerard's picture.

In the month of July, 1785, Father Mansione assisted in his last moments the notary Fungaroli, who had been attacked by a putrid fever. Suddenly, Pasquale de Silla entered, who, seeing his friend dying, laid on his breast a picture of the venerated Redemptorist, saying: "Brother Gerard, I have heard of the wonders you everywhere perform. But if you do not cure my friend, I will not think you a Saint." At that instant, in Father Mansione's presence, the dying man was completely cured.

One of our brothers was relating to the Marchesa de Granafe incidents of Gerard's life which proclaimed his great simplicity and obedience. The Marchesa, little accustomed to hear such facts, though sometimes met in the lives of the Saints, exclaimed: "Oh, that is enough for me! I see plainly that he was a holy fanatic."

"God grant, madam," replied the brother, "that you may not be obliged one day to have recourse to him who you call a fanatic." Two months had scarcely passed when this lady was seized with a mortal illness and given up by the physicians. In her extremity she turned to Brother Gerard and said, "If you are really a Saint, show it, and I will contribute to your Beatification." Hardly had she made the promise when she was cured.

In 1817, the notary Gualdieri of San Severino was attacked by acute nephritis. In spite of the most energetic remedies, his pains only increased in intensity. He applied a picture of Brother Gerard, begging him to cure him. After his prayer, he fell asleep and saw in a dream the Saint, who by the Sign of the Cross restored him to perfect health.

In 1824, Lady Dorotea Perrotti of Capaccio, attacked by liver and lung trouble, was nearing her end. The priest was reciting the recommendation of her soul when our Brother Raffaello Ricciardi entered. Moved by the profound affliction of the family, he told them to pray to Brother Gerard and he applied to the dying woman a relic of the Saint which he carried about him. Suddenly, Dorotea opened her eyes, asked for a drink and exclaimed: "A favor! A favor!" When questioned, she answered: "I have just seen a religious holding in his hand a lung and a liver entirely diseased, and he said to me: 'See your liver and your lung.'

" 'Who are you?' I asked.

" 'I am Brother Gerard. I have taken away from you your decayed organs, but I have given you another of each. Have courage!'" And instantly Dorotea arose in perfect health.

In 1830, the physician Vitus Federici of Pandola had a tumor in the side so grave that the most celebrated medical authorities, having exhausted their remedies, advised him to receive the Last Sacraments. The sick man then took a picture of Brother Gerard and begged him to cure him in eight days. On the eighth day, though worse than ever, he fell into a light sleep, from which he awoke completely cured, the tumor having disappeared.

The year 1837 was a fatal one for the kingdom of Naples. The cholera claimed innumerable victims. How many cures were then wrought by our thaumaturgus! His Italian biography, after giving a long list of miracles, says that the Saint was the heavenly physician and his picture the most efficacious remedy against the terrible scourge.

Toward 1838, Donna Fungaroli, attacked by consumptive fever, was suddenly cured during her sleep, in consequence of an apparition of Brother Gerard.

In 1843, a barber of Avellino had his cerebral artery cut by the hand of an enemy. He was in his last moments when someone applied to the wound a picture of Brother Gerard. The cure was instantaneous. Even the doctors, who had declared a cure impossible, cried out: "A miracle!"

In 1849, Teresa Deheneffe received a blow of a knife in the left side. For three years the wound was inflamed, so that the physicians decided upon a very dangerous operation. But two days after, they declared the case desperate. Her confessor then advised the sick woman to make a novena to Brother Gerard. While the novena was going on, the linens and the plaster fell off of themselves, and the physicians found the wound cured. There was not the least trace of a scar, although on the previous evening the wound was still open and frightful to behold.

In 1856, Frederic Thormayer, an employee in an iron factory near Aix-la-Chapelle, had a foot frightfully burned and dislocated by the fall of a piece of red-hot iron. He was taken to a hospital, but the surgeon could not set the bone on account of the horrible burn. For a whole month the unfortunate man uttered cries of pain. One day, his brother, a lay brother in the house of the Redemptorists at

Amsterdam, advised him by letter to put on his foot a picture of Brother Gerard. Frederic hastened to do so. That night he slept for the first time since the accident. The next day, on awakening, he was perfectly cured, to the amazement of the surgeon who had come to amputate the foot.

About this same time, Maria Van Rosiyen, of Werkhoven, Holland, was attacked by dropsy and hemorrhages. After receiving the Last Sacraments, she began a novena to the angelic Gerard, and she was cured in so short a time that the Protestant physician declared that such a cure was above the natural.

In 1858, Ursula Solito, stricken by a frightful cancer, was abandoned by the doctors, who thought it necessary that she receive the Last Sacraments. Her friends placed on her head a picture of the holy Redemptorist and began to pray for her most fervently. Some moments after, Ursula became agitated, complained of having received a violent blow on the forehead, the seat of the disease, and showed signs of very great pain. Soon she fell into a sleep. On awakening, she saw around her the doctors who, utterly amazed, proclaimed her perfectly cured. "It is not you who have cured me," she said to them laughing, "it is Brother Gerard."

In 1865, Andrea Cattaldi of Alatri received a stiletto wound in the stomach during a brawl. The wound was between three and four inches in depth and about one and a half inches long. The wounded man was at once laid on a bed, and a surgeon came to dress the wound. When he had finished, Andrea laid on the wound *The Life of Brother Gerard.* The next day, the doctor of science having returned, he found the wound so well closed that, seeing the Life of the Saint lying on the bed, he exclaimed: "There is the one who has cured you!"

In 1874, the holy brother cured a medical student of Naples, who had been ill of cancerous diphtheria.

E. Prodigies in Favor of Children

THE Saint, himself simple and innocent as a child, showed special predilection for children. We shall cite some facts.

A son of Christina de Rogatis was for several months consumed by a slow fever accompanied by a flow of blood. One morning, he was found dead in his bed. The inconsolable mother had recourse to Brother Gerard. Applying a tooth of the Servant of God to the corpse, she cried: "Brother Gerard, do not abandon me in my grief. Restore my son to life!" On the instant, the child resuscitated, opened his eyes and arose full of life and health.

A child between four and five years old, the nephew of the Lords Ilario, was attacked in July, 1781 by a mortal fever. Alarmed at his state, the family invoked the Servant of God. One night, the child cried out joyously: "Mama, Mama, see Brother Gerard! See how beautiful he is! how shining! Mama, get up! Come, see!" And then he added: "Oh, he is gone!" Next day, the child arose perfectly cured.

Father Tannoia relates that a little girl of Senerchia had died. In her extreme affliction, the mother had recourse with confidence to the Saint, applying his picture to the dead body of her dear child. At once, to the amazement of all present, the child began to speak, then to eat and to play, as if she had never been sick.

In 1829, little Agata Flavia of Caposele, about two years old, suffered from so violent a convulsive cough that her parents were deeply distressed. At last they recommended her to Brother Gerard. Suddenly, the child exclaimed: "I see Brother Gerard! I see Brother Gerard!" She was cured. Her mother, inebriated with joy, showed her different pictures. The little one instantly put her finger on that of the Saint: "There is the one who cured me!"

In 1830, Agnese Forlenza of Caposele, a child of six years, fell seriously ill and gave so little hope of a cure that preparations for her funeral were already thought of. At the very moment that she was about to breathe her last, they laid on her a relic of Brother Gerard. Immediately, the little dying child cried out: "I am cured! Brother Gerard has cured me!" The doctor declared it a miracle.

In 1831, Vincenzo Flavio, being absent from his family, learned that his daughter Rafaelle was on the point of suffocating with diphtheria. Vincenzo, who had with him the *Life of Brother Gerard,* tore out the Saint's picture and, holding it in his hand, said: "Brother Gerard, now is the time to show your sanctity." Noting the hour, he hastily turned his steps homeward. When he entered the house, he found his child cured. The cure had been effected at the precise moment that he had invoked the Saint. This miracle was followed by another still greater. Vincenzo obtained through Brother Gerard the grace to lay aside a mortal hatred which he had long nourished.

In 1833, a young child named Giuseppe Dorsi of Calvanico had sores upon the head which the doctors considered incurable. His mother applied to him a picture of the Saint. Ten minutes later the child said: "I want to get up. I am cured."

"But how?" cried the mother in great astonishment and emotion.

"Brother Gerard came in by this window," answered the happy child. "He came to my bed, laid his hand on my head and exclaimed: 'A cure! A cure! A cure!' and then disappeared."

In 1853 there occurred the cure of Vincenzo d'Onfrio of Naples. This child, aged eight years, had been frightfully burned in the face by setting fire accidentally to a little bag of powder.

In 1865, a physician of Luxembourg, Belgium had a son aged four years who could neither walk nor talk. A man of faith, he had just read *The Life of Brother Gerard*. Charmed by the wonders he had read and saddened to see his child seated on the floor at his side crippled and mute, he exclaimed, "Brother Gerard, show your power and cure my son present here." At that instant, the little fellow rose up and ran to his father, saying, "Papa." From that time onward the child spoke and walked like other children of his age.

In 1867, Lorenzo Riola, a child of ten, after being given up by the most distinguished physicians of Naples, begged his cure from Brother Gerard. The child fell asleep and dreamed that he saw a golden ladder which, resting on his head, rose up to Heaven. On the ladder he saw descending Brother Gerard, holding on his left arm a Crucifix. The holy religious touched the child, who instantly arose perfectly cured.

F. Prodigies in Favor of Mothers

WE cannot end this part of our work without speaking of the marvelous privilege which God seems to have imparted to our Saint, namely, that of protecting mothers and children in the numerous dangers that accompany maternity. There are some counties where there is not a mother who does not have his picture and who does not devoutly invoke his name.

The special gift which God seems to have given His great servant for cases of this kind was very frequently manifested even in his own lifetime. It will suffice to mention the following facts:

A woman of Senerchia was about to die. In the desperate state in which the sick woman lay, her friends had recourse to Gerard, who promised to pray for her. Hardly had he done so when the tears of the family were turned to joy.

As Gerard came out one day from a house at Oliveto, a young girl hurried after him with a handkerchief which he had inadvertently left on a chair. "Keep it," said the admirable and faithful servant of Christ, "it will be useful to you some day." The girl married and was in fact on the point of dying with her first child. In her extremity, she called for the handkerchief of the pious Redemptorist. The danger instantly passed and with it even the pains incidental to her condition.

But it is above all since his death that the Saint has shown himself the protector of maternity.

A child born at Oliveto died immediately after Baptism. In their grief, the parents, Tomaso Ronco and his wife, implored Gerard's help, making at the same time an application of his relics to their child. Oh, prodigy! At that instant the babe began to breathe. It was saved.

In 1795, a young woman of Benevento belonging to the Cocca family, being reduced to extremity, had recourse to Brother Gerard and had a picture of the Servant of God laid on her head. That night, the Brother appeared to her in the Redemptorist habit. "Courage," he said, "you are cured." The next morning the physicians, to their great surprise, found her in a state of perfect health.

The limits of space which we have prescribed to ourselves force us to omit a multitude of miraculous deliveries which the biographies of the holy Brother have handed down to us.

Since his Beatification in January, 1893, numbers

of similar favors have been obtained. Several of these have been related in *La Sainte-Famille (The Holy Family)* and in *La Voix du Redempteur (The Voice of the Redeemer)*.

G. Beatification and Further Miracles

INNUMERABLE favors have been daily added to the list of those we have mentioned.

On January 26, 1892 in our church of Nocera there took place the Exposition of the Most Blessed Sacrament to obtain the Beatification of the Servant of God. A woman who had a horrible sore on her head that was extremely painful and had been pronounced incurable went to the church and exclaimed with lively faith: "Brother Gerard, if you are a Saint, cure me!" She was instantly and completely cured. Two physicians attested in writing to the wonderful cure.

On June 26, 1856, ecclesiastical authority, desiring to recognize and examine the relics of the Servant of God, had his tomb opened for the first time. Now, as one after the other, the head and other bones were deposited in a vessel prepared to receive them, there was seen to ooze from them a mysterious perfumed oil in such abundance that the basin was filled with it, and it even ran over. This marvelous *manna*, as the Italians call it, was gathered up with great care on handkerchiefs and linens, of which the sick soon attested the power.

On October 11, 1892, the precious remains were

again taken from the sepulcher to be examined by ecclesiastical authority in the presence of two physicians. The bones were found more or less humid, but since this phenomenon might be attributed to the dampness of the ground, no attention was paid to it. They were carefully dried and enclosed in a casket ornamented with white silk. Four hours later, the casket was opened. A kind of white oil of a sweet odor was oozing from the holy relics and lying like drops of dew on the silk lining.

After a very rigorous examination, the physicians drew up an official report of the fact, which according to their judgment, surpassed the natural order. "It is needless to say what joy this prodigy caused us!" exclaimed the narrator. "It is without doubt a presage of the favors that the holy Brother wishes to shed upon those who honor him."

Lastly, in the morning of January 29, 1893, under the generalate of the Most Rev. Father Nicolo Mauron, the ceremony of Beatification took place amid the acclamations a thousand times repeated: *"Viva Leone XIII!"* ("Long live Leo XIII!") This day did not pass without new prodigies.

According to custom, the Holy Father and the faithful went in the afternoon to venerate the relics of the newly Beatified and to pray before his picture. Now at two o'clock the vast hall of Beatification was crowded. The three thousand candles, which make of this beautiful hall a true Paradise of glory, were being lighted. An employee of the Vatican, Augusto Scarpellini, mounted on a ladder forty-five feet high, was lighting the candles around the picture of Blessed Gerard. Suddenly, a cry escaped from every lip, a noise of broken chandeliers was heard. The ladder having slipped to one side, the unfortunate Scarpellini lost his balance and fell head foremost into space. The multitude instantly raised their hands to the Saint with the cry: *"Santo, Santo Gerado! Santo!"* "Saint! Saint Gerard! Saint!" It was an indescribable but never to be forgotten moment. Suddenly the ladder struck a chandelier, which made it rebound to the other side, overturning all the candelabras of the altar, and Scarpellini, instead of being dashed to the pavement, was thrown off into a tribune. They thought him dead, and they rushed to see. But, oh, marvel! He arose safe and sound. They cried out: "A miracle!" They thanked the *Beato*. Joy shone on every face and overflowed all hearts.

This prodigy, and many others that followed the Beatification, influenced the Holy See. On the petition of several cardinals and bishops, the Holy Father, Pope Leo XIII, permitted by a decree dated June 27, 1893 the cause of Canonization of Blessed Gerard to be pursued. In the petition to this effect addressed to His Holiness, the following prodigies are cited:

1. The almost instantaneous cure of a sick man who was as the point of death in consequence of severe colic and who had been given up by the physicians.

2. The unexpected delivery of a mother and the raising to life of her dead child.

3. The raising to life of another child, preparations for whose funeral had already been made.

4. The cure of a consumptive religious sister.

5. The instantaneous disappearance of an ulcer from the finger of a Sister of Charity at the moment when amputation was decided to be necessary.

To these later favors, we add the following, obtained in 1893:

Not far from the convent of Pagani, in which St. Alphonsus died, a holy priest had experienced the affliction of losing in a short time his father, mother, brothers and sisters. All had been suddenly carried away after several days' severe sickness. The priest feared that he too would die in the same way. And in fact, shortly after the Beatification of Blessed Gerard, he felt himself attacked by the same strange sickness, the fatal sign of a speedy death. We may imagine the consternation of the sick man. Then he conceived the idea of praying to our Saint. Filled with gloomy presentiments, he retired to rest. During his sleep, at a moment when it seemed to him he was about to expire, he beheld coming toward him Brother Gerard, who said: "What do you want of me?"

"O good brother," responded the priest, "I beg you not to let me die suddenly."

"Why no," replied Blessed Gerard, "you will not die. But I want you to take to our Fathers at Pagani the sum of two hundred francs, that they may devote them to the expenses of my Canonization." This said, he disappeared. On awakening, the priest found that he was perfectly cured, and he very willingly sent to the Fathers the sum indicated.

A good carpenter went with his wife to the same convent of Pagani to ask for a picture of Blessed Gerard. Having obtained it, he kissed it several times with fervid Italian devotion and promised to frame it for an ornament in his home. While waiting to do so, he put it away in a drawer. Unfortunately, when taking something out of the drawer, his wife tore the picture in two. Distressed at the accident and fearing a violent scene, she hid the torn picture from her husband, locking it in a chest. Every time he mentioned it, she changed the subject, thinking to make him forget it. But in vain. Though so safely hidden away, it was no less present to his memory. One day, he demanded in a decided tone his cherished picture. The poor woman, seeing that the time had passed for lending a deaf ear, began in tears to relate the story of the sad accident. We may imagine the husband's chagrin. Restraining his anger, however, he insisted on seeing the remains of his precious treasure. Together they opened the chest. Wonderful to relate, the picture was whole again. But on examining it more closely, they noticed the trace of the tear, though on the back only. It looked like a very fine thread or fish bone. "A miracle! A miracle!" cried both husband and wife with one voice. The neighbors ran in at the cry, surrounding them, interrogating them, examining the mysterious object and shedding tears of emotion. And that was not all. The Bishop of the diocese heard the report about Blessed Gerard's picture. He wished to see it and to hear the marvelous fact from the favored couple themselves. But what was the amazement of the latter when, placing the venerated picture in the hands of the prelate, they found that every trace of the tear had disappeared! The witnesses confirmed under oath the authenticity of this prodigy.

A young woman was carrying on a business, which threatened to fail. Five thousand francs had to be raised at any cost. It was impossible for her to collect the sum; her every attempt was fruitless. She made a novena to Saint Gerard. The third day, her sales were numerous; the fifth, still more so; and, at the end of the novena, she had all that she needed.

A gentleman was in great need of money. Someone advised him to make a novena in honor of Blessed Gerard, and he began to do so with confidence. During the novena, he won a prize that relieved him of his financial embarrassment.

Sister Lorenza, *Fille de la Sagesse* (a Daughter of Wisdom) of Ghlin, had for months been suffering from caries of the jawbone. The infection of the wound was such as to keep the patient sick. One doctor declared an operation necessary, but another undertook to cure her by means of antiseptic injections. The disease ever on the increase, the religious turned to Blessed Gerard, promising a novena of Communions in his honor if she were cured. The linens being removed one morning, an insupportable stench filled the room, but the sister was completely cured. This cure took place on October 5, 1893.

The Sisters of Mercy of Liège have for their principal occupation the making of rich ornaments for the altar. By an unforeseen accident, a very perceptible stain was produced on a chasuble of precious gold cloth. "As we knew by experience that nothing could remove it," said Sister Maria Kostka, who relates the fact, "it occurred to me to apply a relic of Blessed Gerard Majella, which, fortunately, we had then at hand. I made the sisters and pupils present in the workroom pray for the favor desired. Then I lightly passed the relic over the stain in the presence of another sister. Surprised and wondering, we saw it instantly disappearing before our eyes, excepting at one place, over which I vainly passed the relic. Now, how it was I do not know, but precisely over that place would necessarily pass the galloon (the ornamented band) and thus hide the rest of the stain." Is it not touching to see how the saintly Brother hastens to the help of those who invoke him, even in the little everyday difficulties of life?

A "Black Sister" (*Soeur Noire*) of Mons for five months endured the intense pains of arthritis in her right knee. Any movement of the knee was impossible. Remedies proving fruitless, she was advised to invoke Blessed Gerard. It was on September 6. This was the simple prayer that she offered: "Brother Gerard, please to cure me, and be quick about it, or I shall ask my cure of the Blessed Virgin the day after tomorrow, the feast of her Nativity. Spare her this trouble." That evening, she placed on the suffering part the picture of the Servant of God. Oh, what happiness! Next morning, on awakening, she found herself completely cured. She was able to rise, go to the chapel, make a genuflection and approach the Holy Table with the same ease as if she had never known suffering.

A woman by the name of Coppens-Bastiaens of Brussels had been suffering from chronic bronchitis for twenty-one years. Night and day she was tormented by a cough, and four times had she received the Last Sacraments. At the approach of the solemnities which were to take place in the Redemptorist church on *rue de la Madeleine* for the Beatification of Brother Gerard, she felt arise in her soul a great desire to assist at the service. But her malady, instead of decreasing, became so aggravated that they thought of again giving her Extreme Unction. Then it was that, filled with confidence, she made this short prayer: "Blessed Brother Gerard, you work so many miracles and you cure so many sick people; deign to cure me also, that I may be able to assist with my husband at your triduum [three days of prayer]." At that moment an interior voice said to her: "Well then, get up! You are cured." And she, full of faith, exclaimed: "I am cured!" Her husband thought her delirious. But without more ado, she arose and dressed. On October 15, the first day of the triduum, she went to church, received Holy Communion and, in short, spent six hours there without experiencing the least fatigue.

A lady of Antwerp suffered for five years from a

horrible purulent wound on her leg above the ankle. The tibial bone was laid bare, as if the flesh had been eaten by cancer. All the remedies employed were without success, and the pain was intolerable. The bandages had to be changed three or four times a day. One day, the doctor declared that the patient must be removed to a hospital, and it was feared he had decided on amputation. It was at this moment that the family thought of praying to Blessed Gerard. They began a novena in his honor, applying his relic to the diseased limb. From the very first day, a noticeable relief was felt, and on the eighth day the cure was complete. The lady took off the bandages and began to attend to the affairs of her household, assuring her friends that she had never felt better.

Sister Françoise-Marguerite, a religious of the Visitation near Ghent in Belgium, had suffered for ten months from articular rheumatism, which caused her insupportable pains. Two physicians had vainly tried to relieve her. Hearing of the miracles performed by Blessed Gerard, she made a novena in his honor to obtain her cure. But her confidence was put to the test. Two days before the close of the novena, her pains were so intense that the poor sister, in spite of her courage, groaned and shed tears for two and a half hours. On the last day of the novena, the pain suddenly ceased. A miraculous cure had taken place.

At Santiago, Chili, some days after a solemn triduum in honor of Blessed Gerard, a messenger came to beg one of our Fathers to pay a visit to a very distinguished man of the city, notorious for his impiety and connection with the Freemasons. The priest was well received and was conducted into a drawing room in which was a large picture of the holy Redemptorist with a lamp burning before it. "What is the meaning of this lamp and this picture?" exclaimed the religious. "Ah! Father," answered the Freemason, "be not surprised at what you see. It is because of this good Saint that my wife and I are thinking of being converted." Then he began to tell that, having heard during the triduum of the miraculous power attributed to Brother Gerard, he thought he would test it by asking two favors of him. One day, having gone on his richly harnessed horse to the station, he alighted for a few minutes, during which time the horse disappeared. Search was at once made in all directions, but no horse could be found. Eight days passed, during which a new accident happened. His wife lost a ring valued at six hundred dollars. Now, it was this horse and ring that the gentleman had asked Blessed Gerard to restore. After these eight days, he had occasion to return to the station, and what was his amazement to find his horse at the same place where he had tied it a week before, the harness complete and in good condition! He asked for information and learned that the horse had come on a southern train. He could never discover anything more. But that was not all. On returning home, he passed through the garden where his wife was, for he was eager to show her his horse. But she, frightened by the prancing of the animal, drew back and fell. In her fall, her hand slipped under a plant and came into contact with something solid. Oh, wonder! It was her precious ring! In consequence of this double favor, the couple vowed to Blessed Gerard their liveliest gratitude, which led to their sincere return to God.

The following fact took place at the orphanage of the Ladies of the Blessed Sacrament, Watermael, near Brussels. A young girl of seventeen named Juliette Denis had suffered for almost two years from inflammation in the knees. The slightest touch on the knees—what do I say?—even the shaking of the floor under a heavy footstep in her room caused her intolerable suffering and made her cry for mercy. A Redemptorist priest engaged the orphans to ask the cure of this poor girl from Brother Gerard, to whom they made a novena preparatory to his feast. They did so fervently. On the day of the feast, the poor invalid was taken to the oratory to hear Mass and receive Holy Communion. Suddenly, Juliette felt herself cured, arose and went up boldly to the altar with her companions. When the Mass was over, she deposited her crutches at the feet of Blessed Gerard. In his certificate of cure, the physician says: "Although we regard ancholysis as incurable, the joints have unexpectedly and instantaneously regained their suppleness, and at the same time the pains have disappeared."

Dominico Beneducce of Somma Vesuniano was attacked by a terrible malady known by the name of *miserere*. When all hope of saving his life was gone, they applied to him the relics of Blessed Gerard. This was on May 14, 1893. On that same day, which to all appearances was destined to be the last day of his life, Dominico recovered his health.

The cure of a child of two months, little Giuseppina Calabrose, is no less wonderful. A violent sickness had reduced her to extremity, and her little body had become rigid and immovable as a corpse. Her parents, thinking her dead, turned in their desolation to Blessed Gerard. A few instants after, to the joy and amazement of all, the child moved and opened her eyes. Gerard had cured her whose funeral was already being prepared.

All these marvels and many others besides took place in 1893, the year of Brother Gerard's Beatification. Since then the favors obtained by the Saint's intercession are innumerable. God is evidently pleased to exalt His humble servant. A large volume would not suffice to record all the prodigies that have come to our knowledge. Above all, the confidence of [expectant] mothers in danger is recompensed. Physicians have declared that many of these desperate cases succeeded only by a miracle. In six months, our house of Liège alone received over a hundred and twenty thanksgivings relative to this subject.

We give here some other miracles chosen from a thousand:

Mgr. Wulfingh, Bishop of Surinam, relates the following fact: The wife of a physician fell dangerously ill in April, 1895, about ten days after the birth

of her child. Her husband called in three other doctors, and all agreed that the resources of medicine
were insufficient to ward off death from the patient,
and soon indeed her agony began. Already the
extremities were cold, the face and hands, attacked
by decomposition, became black. The doctors said:
"All will be over in five minutes." Just at that
moment, there entered the room a pious lady possessing a picture and a relic of Blessed Gerard.
Unknown to those present, she applied them to the
dying woman. The latter immediately opened her
eyes, saying that she was cured. The four physicians,
all Protestants, after verifying the cure, declared it
absolutely marvelous.

The following fact happened at Buga, Colombia.
A child of three years, playing with his brother on
the bank of a river, fell in. The older one ran at once
to apprise the mother of the accident. She immediately invoked Blessed Gerard and flew to the spot
where the child had disappeared. She sought him
anxiously and in tears. A half hour passed, when
suddenly she found her child. Humanly speaking, he
should have been dead. But no, the hand of Gerard
had saved him. Ever after, the good mother recounted
to every newcomer that her son owed his life to the
charitable Servant of God.

A young lady of Sainte-Marie de la Beauce,
Canada suffered for five months the total loss of her
voice and violent stomach trouble. The last day of
a novena to the Blessed, she went to bed worse than
ever, earnestly commending herself to him whom

she called the great friend of the Sacred Heart. On rising, she found herself so perfectly cured that she began to cry out: "Thank you, Brother Gerard!" Thenceforth she proclaimed to all the praises of her benefactor.

A religious of Rimouski, Canada was dying of consumption. She could hardly digest some spoonfuls of broth. Rev. Father Tielen, who was giving the exercises of the retreat to the religious, went to the infirmary to hear her Confession. On leaving, he lent her his relic of Blessed Gerard. The next day, the invalid felt her strength suddenly return and cried out: "I am cured! I am cured!" The doctor certified a perfect cure, and the sister, full of strength, readily resumed her class duties without experiencing the least fatigue.

In 1894, a woman from the environs of Saint-Nicolas-du-Port came to pay a visit to one of our priests with her little daughter, eight years old. The Father noticed that the child carried her head firmly resting on one shoulder. "What is the matter with your child?" inquired the priest.

"For over a year," answered the mother, "she has had an abscess which suppurates constantly and prevents her moving her head."

"Ah!" replied the religious, "we must obtain the cure of this little one by a novena to Blessed Gerard." A few days after, the same lady again presented herself at the convent, with her little girl joyfully skipping by her side. "Ah, well," said the priest, "what news?"

"My daughter is cured. She was cured instantaneously at the end of the novena. See, there remains not even a trace of the abscess."

Among the infirmities of humanity, there is one which seems more than any other to arouse the compassion of the great thaumaturgus, and that is epilepsy. How many epileptics declare that they owe their thorough cure to him!

A lady of Liège had suffered from this malady for over thirty years. Since she began to invoke the charitable brother, she declares that she has not had one relapse.

A woman of Antwerp was for twelve years subject to this terrible sickness. On October 2, 1894, she promised Blessed Gerard to attribute to him her cure and to publish it if, for a whole year, she had no attack. On October 3, 1895, she fulfilled her promise, having had no relapse during the year.

We know of some admirable conversions effected by the Saint during life, but I know not whether those that he still brings about under our eyes are not more astonishing. We behold sinners returning to God after ten, twenty, thirty years of wandering.

A woman of Liège lived for over thirty years in all kinds of moral disorders and horrible sacrileges. On several Mondays she went to the Mass celebrated in honor of Blessed Gerard and soon conceived such remorse for her sins that she could not sleep. She was forced to throw herself at the feet of a priest, to whom she made her Confession with torrents of tears. "It is to the saintly Brother Gerard," she said, "that I owe this grace."

After a life of forgetfulness of God and his duties, a person of Liège was at the point of death. A pious young girl devoted to Blessed Gerard, hearing of the case, hastened to send a medal of the glorious Brother to the nurse in charge of the dying man, that she might place it somewhere around his bed. The next day the sinner, an out-and-out socialist, several times called for a priest, gave him a gracious welcome when he came, received the Last Sacraments in the most Christian sentiments, declared that he wanted to be buried with the rites of our holy Religion and even expressed the desire to have three priests at his funeral rites.

A young man of Brest was dying of lung trouble. He was one of those unfortunates who had pledged himself to die without the Sacraments and to be interred with only civil ceremonies. Happily, a very pious woman did violence to our Blessed Brother on his behalf, and thanks to her prayers, a complete change was suddenly effected in the poor invalid. He welcomed a priest, made his Confession and died in the best sentiments.

A Little Sister of the Poor relates the following conversion. An aged Englishman, an enemy to every religious practice, had already voluntarily assisted at five retreats without showing signs of conversion. The hardened sinner fell ill, and a novena to Blessed Gerard was at once begun for him. On the ninth day, he asked to become a Catholic, and from that time a complete change took place in him. Prayer became his element, and soon he had the happiness of receiving Baptism and First Communion.

A seamstress of Saint-Trond was attacked by pulmonary consumption. Already the right lung was gone, and the left was seriously affected. Day and night was she harassed by a violent cough and purulent expectorations of a fetid odor. The physician pronounced death inevitable, and the sick woman knew it herself. Discarding all human remedies, she confidently turned to Blessed Gerard, paying him, although with the most painful effort, several visits in our church of Saint-Trond. At last, one morning after her devotions, she arose entirely and perfectly cured. The physician, after subjecting her to a thorough examination, had no difficulty in declaring that her cure was a prodigy of the first order and unheard-of in the annals of science.

From Antwerp we received the following account: In the early months of 1894, an infant of three months was attacked by a sickness so grave that the doctor declared there was no hope of a cure. The parents, distracted with sorrow, saw the sad prediction realized. The infant soon breathed its last. In vain did they hold a mirror to its lips. Respiration had ceased. When the little corpse was cold, they washed and prepared it for burial. At that moment, the mother bethought herself of the miracles effected by Blessed Gerard. She applied a relic and a picture of the Servant of God to her beloved child and then, full of confidence fell on her knees by its side and said a fervent prayer. That done, she was obliged to go downstairs for something. A little later, her husband went to take his last leave of the child they were so soon to consign to the grave. When he reached the head of the stairs, he heard some movement in the room. He entered quickly and found his child returned to life. He is at this moment a robust boy to whom they have given the name of Gerard. Wishing to assure himself of a fact so marvelous, one of our priests visited the house of the parents to obtain the exact details.

A lady of Louvain suffering from a dangerous hernia was instantaneously cured by the application of a relic of Blessed Gerard. The physician recognized the miraculous character of the cure.

A lady of Liège was attacked by double pneumonia. A female relative, seeing her lying unconscious, laid a picture of the Saint on her breast. The next day, the invalid was entirely freed from suffering, to the great surprise of the physician.

Another lady of Liège was subject to frequent fainting spells caused by nervous congestion, derangement of the stomach and inflammation of the throat. She made a novena to Blessed Gerard, but on the eighth day, she was worse than ever. On the ninth, however, she felt herself perfectly cured, and the doctor declared that he had never seen her so well.

A very marvelous fact—as related by witnesses—took place at N., a village some miles from Liège. An infant had died without Baptism, or at least appearances so plainly pointed that way that the physician thought it useless to waste his care upon the child. The mother, a profoundly Christian woman, was in the depths of affliction. She began confidently to invoke our dear Blessed Brother, promising, if he would deign to recall her child to life, that she would give it in Baptism the name of Gerard. Her prayer was heard, for soon the child gave signs of life. Today this little Gerard is growing wonderfully.

In 1896, the Superioress of the convent of Herenfeld had to put up new buildings for the school, but when it was time to pay the debt contracted, funds were short. One gentleman alone knew of the distress of the house. To find some means out of their financial distress, the community made a novena to Blessed Gerard, who had miraculously procured so much money for the construction of the convent of Caposele. During the novena, the Superioress received a package. She opened it and drew from it a bill for one hundred marks, about $25, then a second, and third, a tenth, a twentieth, etc. She drew out just as much as was needed to defray the debt, which was considerable. She hastened to thank the gentleman of whom we have made mention, under the impression that the gift came from him. But he declared that he had absolutely nothing to do with it. It was, then, a favor granted by Blessed Gerard, and what follows is an evident proof of it. A piano was needed for the pupils. The Superioress said: "Let us ask Blessed Gerard for it by a novena." During the novena, a lady who had lost her only

daughter came to seek among the sisters a little consolation. All at once, the lady said: "I have a beautiful piano on which my poor child loved to amuse
herself. I cannot bear to look at it. If you wish, I
shall make you a present of it." It is needless to
describe the wonder, joy and gratitude of the community on seeing this new proof of Blessed Gerard's
kindness.

Also in 1896, a brother of our Congregation, still
a novice, had lost his hearing, and every human remedy had been resorted to in vain. The Superior had
to tell him that he could not be admitted to the holy
vows, which decision came like a thunderbolt on the
good brother. He begged the Father Rector to keep
him for nine days longer, that he might with his parents make a novena to Blessed Gerard for his cure.
On the last day of the novena, when sweeping the
corridors, the brother heard the community bell ring.
Was he cured? Was he dreaming? Soon he heard the
clock strike the hour. He ran immediately to the
Superior, crying: "I am cured! I hear! Brother Gerard
has cured me!" The good brother from Heaven had
effectively heard the suppliant prayers of his brother
on earth.

Lady Salvatore Sabatino de Gragnano of Naples
was for two years afflicted by some internal trouble that caused her untold suffering. She was visibly fading away. Two of the best practitioners of
Naples were consulted, who declared that an operation was not only necessary, but even urgent.
Distressed at this news, the good lady turned to

Blessed Gerard, promising, if he would cure her, to give to him the value of her precious clothes and to wear for the future only what was very plain and of a dark color. She was heard. Her prayer was so perfectly granted that the physician declared that he found her in a state of perfect health. Filled with gratitude, she distinguishes herself today (1896) by her zeal in spreading devotion to Blessed Gerard.

Mr. Edmond Zemblay, a Canadian seaman, had to struggle on October 25, 1895 against a furious tempest. The wind was so violent that the schooner could not be steered. Increasing the danger, another schooner, also tempest-tossed, was rapidly approaching. Each threatened the other with destruction; shipwreck seemed imminent. In their extreme peril, the captain remembered that he had a picture of Blessed Gerard, and he said to his companions: "If Blessed Gerard can do something for us, now is the time to show us his power with God." Together they prayed. Instantly the tempest ceased, and they took refuge in the port of Bic-Mein. The two vessels were hardly in safety when the tempest began again more violently than ever. All felt sure that without Gerard's protection both vessels would have been engulfed.

A man of Antwerp in 1896 suffered for over a year from a horrible cancer on his face, near the brain. His pains were unspeakable. The physician judged the cancer incurable. After a severe operation, the cancer put out new roots. The patient refused to undergo a second operation and began confidently to invoke Blessed Gerard. One morning, he perceived that a piece of flesh almost two inches long and one inch wide had fallen from his face. He was cured, and so perfectly as to retain no mark of the disease.

In the same year, little Gerard Vivegnis of Liège had been consecrated before his birth to our dear Thaumaturgus. The child, only nine months old, fell head foremost, I know not by what chance, into a pail of cold water. The mother, entering after a short absence, saw what had happened. She quickly picked up her child, crying in tears: "Blessed Gerard, restore to me my child! Blessed Gerard, save my child!" The little one was cold and blue and gave no sign of life. At the cries of the mother, the neighbors came running in. They began to rub the little drowned babe and to breathe into its mouth. This lasted over an hour, the mother constantly repeating: "Blessed Gerard, restore life to my child!" As death appeared certain, the father, who was laboring at some distance, had to be informed. They were on the point of doing so when the child opened its eyes and began to laugh and act as if nothing had happened to it. Imagine the mother's joy and the gratitude of the family toward Blessed Gerard!

A lady of Brussels had for eighteen years endured a very painful malady. The physicians consulted declared their inability to cure her. Having nothing to hope for from men on earth, the sick woman turned to Blessed Gerard.

On October 16, 1896, on the feast of the holy friend of God, she was completely cured. Since then, she has had not one hour of suffering. They call her Blessed Gerard's miracle.

The following cure took place in Brussels in 1897. A boy of eight years was attacked by pneumonia, complicated with meningitis and congestion. Seeing the frightful convulsions of the child, prolonged sometimes for several hours, the physicians declared that he had but two hours to live. Already the symptoms of approaching death appeared, the eyes were sunken, the lips livid, the extremities cold and black. The parents, frantic with grief, turned to Blessed Gerard and laid on the child his relic. Instantly the little dying one fell asleep—the sleep of restoration—and when he awoke, all danger had disappeared.

A superioress of a certain community was very desirous of beautifying the altar of her chapel, and to obtain the means, she had recourse to Blessed Gerard. For this she daily recited before his picture a *Pater, Ave* and three times the *Gloria Patri.* At the end of a year, she said to him: "If it is true, Brother Gerard, that you have such great influence in Heaven and that you love to enhance the glory of the Heart of Jesus, inspire someone to give five hundred francs, and I will renovate this altar." On leaving the chapel, she met most unexpectedly a lady who offered her the exact sum of five hundred francs.

Our readers have not forgotten that the mortal remains of the Saint are reposing at Caposele. On October 16, 1895, the day of his feast, the pilgrims to his tomb, more numerous than ever, expressed by their exclamations, tears and sobs, their love, grat-

itude and confidence toward the holy thaumaturgus.
Ten confessors, constantly at the service of the faithful, could scarcely satisfy their demands.
Innumerable were the Communions. Father
Bozzoatra delivered the panegyric of the holy
Brother. He was ending by an eloquent prayer when
a brilliant light, like a flash of lightning, proceeded
from the chapel where the sacred bones of the great
Servant of God repose. One would have thought that
an incendiary had set fire to the church. After some
moments of interruption, the prodigy was repeated
a second and a third time. At this, the people began
to cry, "A miracle! A miracle!" and to shed tears of
joy. It produced an immense sensation among all
present, who left animated by redoubled confidence
in Blessed Gerard.

The renown of the numberless prodigies performed
by the servant of God has so roused the confidence
of the people that it surpasses all belief. He is everywhere invoked, his picture is asked for everywhere,
and everywhere are instances of his marvelous protection related.

5. CANONIZATION OF ST. GERARD

IT was, as we have said, on the 29th of January,
1893 that the immortal Leo XIII beatified Gerard
Majella. This grand act gave a marvelous impulse to
devotion to the newly Beatified. Known at first in
Italy alone, our Saint was soon invoked and honored
in all countries in which Redemptorist convents exist.

In the Kingdom of Naples, his native country, Blessed Gerard was at once the subject of an enthusiastic act. His statue was raised in many churches, and the inhabitants of Muro, his own city, even dedicated to him one of massive silver.

The veneration of Blessed Gerard extended not less rapidly throughout France, Holland, America and, above all, Belgium. We may say, in fact, of this last country that it is, so to speak, the classic land of devotion to Blessed Gerard.

He became the cherished patron of all the unfortunate. There was no poverty-stricken creature who did not have recourse to him, no sick person who did not invoke him, no mother in danger who did not claim his powerful mediation, no one in affliction who did not pour out to him fervent supplications.

It may be easily understood that devotion so general could not fail to produce the greatest fruit among a believing people. To secure for themselves the special protection of the thaumaturgus, many poor wanderers returned to better sentiments, wept over their moral disorders and began in earnest a sincerely Christian life. These spiritual advantages did not escape the keen observation of His Eminence Cardinal Goossens, Archbishop of Mechlin, as he manifested in the following words his esteem for the salutary devotion: "The innumerable miracles that fill the life of Blessed Gerard, and those obtained in our own day, edify the faithful and inspire them with great confidence in the Blessed Brother. I should like to see him honored in my diocese as the popular saint *par excellence*."

To respond to this apostolic desire of His Eminence, the Belgian Redemptorists had nothing closer to their hearts than to spread devotion to their Blessed Brother. At last a special devotion was established in his honor which—issuing from Saint-Trond as a starting point—extended throughout all the churches attached to our convents. These efforts were blessed by Heaven, and it could be easily seen that the new devotion would soon attract to the churches of the Redemptorist Fathers a truly remarkable number. At Saint-Trond, Liège and Antwerp, the movement was indeed extraordinary; and such was the crowd of devotees on every Monday, the day dedicated to Blessed Gerard, that, to satisfy the pious eagerness of the multitude, the exercises in his honor had to be repeated. Since that time there are celebrated on Monday at Saint-Trond two Masses in honor of Gerard; at Antwerp, three; at Liège, four. In this last city, the number that assist at these Monday Masses is estimated at over 4,000.

Blessed Gerard—is there any need to say it?—has responded to the piety of these devoted clients by favors without number. The reader has already been convinced of this by the numerous facts recorded in the foregoing chapter. "The prodigies attributed to the intercession of Blessed Gerard," wrote one of our Neapolitan Fathers some years ago, "would supply abundant matter for a monthly review. But our apostolic labors do not leave us the leisure necessary for such a publication." This review now actually exists, and every month *Il Gerardo Majella* publishes a number of favors due to the intercession of the Blessed Brother. Many others may also be seen in the pages of *La Sainte-Famille,*[1] *L'Apotre du Foyer,*[2] and *La Voix du Redempteur.*[3] How many are the sick cured, mothers saved, children rescued from death, afflicted consoled, unfortunate sinners led back to duty and virtue! Gerard's contemporaries aver that several volumes would not hold all the wonders wrought by him during the few years that he spent on earth. We may say the same about the marvelous favors which the Blessed Brother has not ceased to proliferate since the honors of Beatification have been decreed to him. The innumerable favors appeared so extraordinary that—only a few months after his Beatification—twenty-four Cardinals, Archbishops and Bishops presented to the Sacred Congregation of Rites earnest petitions that the cause of Canonization should be taken up without delay. They hoped, as one of them, His Grace the Archbishop of Utrecht, declared, that this new glory given to the Blessed Brother would merit new favors for Christian people, just as the honors of Beatification had opened to the faithful an abundant

---

1. *La Sainte-Famille* (The Holy Family), a review published by the Redemptorist Fathers of the Province of Paris.
2. *L'Apôtre du Foyer* (The Apostle of the Foyer), a review published by the Redemptorist Fathers in Lyons.
3. *La Voix du Rédempteur* (The Voice of the Redeemer), a review published by the Belgian Redemptorists.

source of heavenly graces and benedictions. *Quod illi cessit in gloriam, nobis cedit in gratiam.* ("That which yielded glory for him yields grace for us.")

These petitions, as well as the steps taken by Rev. Father Benedetti, Postulator of the Cause, could not fail to lead to a satisfactory result. On June 27, 1893, the Sacred Congregation gave a favorable vote on the question of opening the Cause for Canonization. All that was now needed was the signature of the Sovereign Pontiff, and that was obtained without difficulty. Leo XIII was greatly impressed by the immense number of miracles obtained through the intervention of Blessed Gerard, and as they one day related to him a new favor due to his intercession, he exclaimed: "That humble brother is a very great Saint!" The Holy Father's confidence in Gerard's power was so great that, a few weeks after his Beatification, Cardinal Zigliara having fallen seriously ill, His Holiness immediately ordered a triduum to obtain through the help of the great thamaturgus the cure of that eminent Prince of the Church, if such were the will of God. We cannot wonder, then, that the Sovereign Pontiff signed the Decree, although only six months had elapsed since his august hands had laid upon Gerard's brow the aureole of the Blessed.

This Decree called for a new process. There was no question of subjecting once more to the crucible of a severe and minute examination virtues already examined and pronounced heroic. No. What remained to be done was to ascertain the will of

God in the matter, to inquire whether it would be pleasing to His Divine Majesty for Gerard to take his place in the number of the Saints whom the universal Church honors with public cultus. We say the universal Church since, in what concerns the Blessed, their cultus is ordinarily restricted to the churches of their native city or diocese, and to those of their Order if they are religious.

Now the divine will is manifested by miracles, which are the plain signature of God. The process of the Canonization of the Blessed is principally concerned with the verification of two miracles. The Church, be it well understood, makes no account in such a process of the miracles, however brilliant they may be, that a Saint has performed in his lifetime. Moreover, when there is question of one already beatified, she exacts, in order to pronounce him in the number of the Saints, the proof of the authenticity of at least two miracles wrought since this Beatification. These alone in her eyes can be legitimately interpreted as divine witnesses which proved that God demands the highest honors for His servant.

We know with what extreme prudence the Roman Court proceeds in these causes. It far surpasses in its precautions all that the criminal courts take, even when there is question of life or death. We may judge of this by the following fact:

The celebrated Cardinal Wiseman was once travelling with a Protestant. After discussing various indifferent subjects, the conversation turned to the veneration of the Saints and their miracles. The

Protestant, we may imagine, showed himself skeptical. The Cardinal then handed him some documents of a process of Canonization relative to certain miracles and their proofs. After reading them, the Protestant said: "Your Eminence, if all miracles were as well proved as these, we should have to believe them."

"Ah! Sir," replied the learned prelate, "these miracles, which seem to you so worthy of belief, the Sacred Congregation of Rites has rejected as not being sufficiently established."

A process was then opened at Rome for the examination of the miracles attributed to the intercession of Blessed Gerard. Three were presented, although the rules of the Congregation of Rites require only two.

The first miracle submitted for approval was the instantaneous cure of Dominico Beneducce, which took place on May 13, 1893. This man reduced to the point of death by the terrible colic, known under the name of *miserere,* had invoked Blessed Gerard and swallowed a thread steeped in the mysterious oil that had oozed from the bones of the thaumaturgus. Instantly, the frightful pain disappeared. This miracle, one of those, doubtless, that Cardinal Wiseman's interlocutor would have approved, was rejected by the Sacred Congregation.

Two others remained. The first of these miracles took place in the diocese of Liège. In the year 1893, a young girl of Saint-Trond named Valerie Baerts, totally exhausted, attacked by typhoid fever in its

worst form and a complication of cerebral meningitis, lay in her agony. No human help availed. She
made a vow, recommended herself to the protection
of Blessed Gerard and recovered her usual strength
as if she had never been sick.

The second miracle took place in 1896. A young
man of fifteen, Vincenzo De Geronimo, was devot-
ing himself to the study of literature in the Seminary
of Conza when he fell ill. The malady made such
progress that the patient was soon at the point of
death. The skill of the most able physicians and all
the care lavished on him were powerless. Every
symptom of the disease indicated a fatal issue, when
the relics of Blessed Gerard were laid on his breast.
Instantly, he fell asleep and, wonderful to relate,
awoke cured.

These two miracles were submitted to a most rigorous examination by the Sacred Congregation of
Rites in different sittings held at Rome in 1898, 1899,
1903 and 1904. As usual, the Promoter of the Faith,
who is popularly known under the not very sympa-
thetic title of the *"Devil's Advocate,"* did all in his
power to detract from their value. But the Postulator
of the Cause so perfectly refuted all the keen and
subtle arguments of his adversary that on July 6, 1904,
to the question proposed by Cardinal Ferrata, the
Ponent of the Cause, as to whether the miracles proposed were clear and certain, all the Cardinals present, as also the Consultors, gave a favorable opinion.

The miracles being approved by the Sacred
Congregation, the cause was terminated. The pro-

nouncing of the sentence belongs to the Pope—the judge infallible and without appeal in such matters. Although present at the sitting of July 26, the Sovereign Pontiff desired, according to custom, again to invoke the Spirit of Truth before pronouncing the definitive sentence.

It was finally rendered on the feast of the Assumption, August 15, 1904. Pius X, by a solemn Decree, declared that he "accepted the two miracles proposed," namely, the first, "the instantaneous and perfect cure of Valerie Baerts in the last stage of typhoid fever, along with complication of cerebral meningitis," and the second, "the instantaneous and perfect cure of Vincenzo De Geronimo of pleurisy."

In a second Decree issued on the same day, by a favor as rare as it is precious, Pius X, fulfilling the unanimous desire of the members of the Congregation of the Most Holy Redeemer, declared that they might safely proceed to the solemn Canonization of Blessed Gerard Majella.

We give here some providential coincidences: It was during the novena for the feast of St. Alphonsus that the Congregation of Rites rendered the affirmative Decree concerning the authenticity of the miracles and the question *de tuto* of the Canonization of Blessed Gerard; it was on the feast of the Assumption that the solemn promulgation took place; it was at a time in which the entire Catholic world was celebrating the fiftieth anniversary of the proclamation of the dogma of the Immaculate Conception that the grand ceremonies of his Canonization occurred. A delicate attention of St. Alphonsus toward this illustrious son whom he himself had canonized while living! Precious testimony of Mary's maternal tenderness toward one of her most loving and devoted servants!

We may cite some other remarkable coincidences: On June 8, 1877, Pius IX, on the fiftieth anniversary of his episcopal consecration, published the Decree declaring the virtues of the Venerable Gerard heroic; on the 29th of January, 1893, at the jubilee festival of the fiftieth year of *his* episcopacy, Leo XIII placed the Venerable Brother in the ranks of the Blessed; lastly, on December 11, 1904, only a few days after the jubilee festival of the fiftieth anniversary of the proclamation of the dogma of the Immaculate Conception, Pius X, then gloriously reigning, proceeded to the solemn Canonization of Blessed Gerard!

But it is time to recount the festivities of this ever memorable day.

First, as to the theater of this glorification, the incomparable basilica of St. Peter's of the Vatican: At the entrance, over the portico, was a magnificent inscription artistically framed and richly ornamented, surmounted by the armorial bearings of the Barnabites and the Redemptorists. It recalled the fact that along with Gerard Majella of the Redemptorists, a son of the Order of Barnabites, Alessandro Sauli, was on the same day to receive the honors of Canonization. The following was the epigraph, composed by Msgr. Vincenzo Sardi:

Adeste cives advenae.
Quod Christianae reipublicae bene vertat
Pius X Pontifex Maximus
Alexandro Sauli Episcopo Sodali Barnabitidi
et
Gerardo Maiella Sodali Alphonsiano
Caelitum Sanctorum honores
Inerranti judicio decernit.
Animas Sanctissimas ut catholico nomini pacem
imploratione pariant
Adprecamini.

"Come, citizens and strangers! The Sovereign
Pontiff Pius X (may it redound to the good of the
Church) decrees in his infallible judgment the honors of the Saints to Alessandro Sauli, Bishop, of the
Order of the Barnabites, and to Gerard Majella, son
of St. Alphonsus. Beg these great Saints to obtain
peace for the Church of God!"

Besides this inscription, there was on the facade
of the church an immense canvas, the work of the
Chevalier Salvator Nobili, on which was represented
the glory of the new Saints. The interior of the basilica still retained the magnificent decorations of the
celebration of December 8, the only change being
that the picture of the Immaculate Conception had
been replaced by that of the Most Holy Trinity. All
else remained as it was. As on the grand jubilee day,
the red damask striped with gold draped the pillars;
the Confession of the Prince of the Apostles was

covered with flowers and candelabra; rich pontifical vestments ornamented the statue of St. Peter;
and the whole basilica was illumined by electricity
from the entrance up to the Chair of St. Peter. To
give the number of sconces and chandeliers would
be almost impossible. In one word, the *Osservatore
Romano* said that the amount of light that then bathed
the immense basilica was equivalent to about 45,000
candle-power.

The festivals of the preceding day almost equalling
in brilliancy those of the eight following days, it
might be expected that St. Peter's would be filled
by an immense crowd. Although the portals were
not to be thrown open until 6:30, the square of St.
Peter's was covered with people from 5:00 a.m.
Order was maintained outside the church by mili-
tary cordons and inside by the Swiss guard and the
sampietrini, who had received orders absolutely to
refuse entrance to anyone not provided with a ticket.
Over fifty thousand persons took places in the vast
body of the temple! One detail was touching: in a
tribune, mingled with the family of St. Alessandro
Sauli, were the members of that of St. Gerard,
namely M. Gerardo Majella, a printer of Tivoli,
Roman States, with his son, Leandro, his daughter
Ersili, and Msgr. Pacifici, a priest of Tivoli.

The immense crowd awaited for some time the
coming of the Sovereign Pontiff. At last was heard
in the distance the sound of voices approaching, and
soon after, an imposing procession began to descend
the royal staircase leading to the basilica. It was

almost 8:30. The procession was formed of three principal sections: the regular clergy, the secular clergy and the papal court.

According to custom, the two religious families who were celebrating the glory of one of their own members led the procession. The other Religious Orders followed: the Jesuits, the barefooted Augustinians, the Capuchins, the Minims, the Conventuals, the Hermits of St. Augustine, the discalced Carmelites, the Dominicans, the Benedictines, the Camaldolese, etc., etc.

Then came the secular clergy of the collegiate basilicas and parishes of Rome, the Prelates of the Vicariate and of the Sacred Congregation of Rites, followed by six Redemptorist religious preceding the banner of their confrere. This was the work of Signore Gagliardi. It was surrounded by numerous pilgrims from Gerard's country.

Behind the secular clergy walked the stately cortege of the pontifical chapel, with the ecclesiastical and lay dignitaries, among whom was the pontifical jeweller. Next came the private clerks bearing the pontifical tiaras and the precious mitre of the Sovereign Pontiff. Then followed the colleges of the prelature; the bearers of the tiara and the mitre which were to be used by the Pope during the ceremony; the bearers of the papal cross, of the censer; the ostiari, doorkeepers, *virga rubea* ("red sceptre"); two penitentiaries, each carrying a rod ornamented with flowers, emblems of their authority; the Abbots-General in their copes, the Bishops to the number of about 200; the Archbishops, Primates, Patriarchs, among whom were the Greek Melchite Prelates, clothed in their rich oriental ornaments; the Cardinal-deacons, the Cardinal-priests, the Cardinal-bishops, wearing their damask mitres, and every one bearing the insignia of his order. Exclusive of the officiating Cardinals, thirty-five Princes of the Church figured in the procession!

The Pope, crowned with the tiara, borne on the *sedia gestatoria,* surrounded by the high ecclesiastical and lay dignitaries of his court, made his entry at 9:15. It had taken three quarters of an hour for the procession to file in. The Holy Father appeared to all surrounded by that superhuman splendor which gives to mortal man the character of the Father of Catholicity and the Vicar of Jesus Christ. Ah, if the multitude could have applauded in testimony of love and inviolable attachment to the successor of St. Peter, to the Pontiff-King! But every noisy manifestation, especially all cheering, had been prohibited. Nevertheless, hardly did the Pontiff appear before the immense crowd was thrilled with emotion. A long murmur of admiration ran through all ranks. They were, at last, gazing on the Pope whose august features they had so longed to behold! The emotion increased when the Supreme Pontiff, himself visibly moved, raised his hand to bless the reverent crowd, while the silver trumpets sent to the four corners of the temple the brilliant notes and cadences of the Longhi march.

As eyewitnesses testified, the festival of the 11th

of December, like that of the 8th, surpassed all that has been witnessed in Rome since the Vatican Council [Vatican I, 1870]. Can we doubt it? It may be seen by what we have said that the pontifical procession displayed under exceptional conditions its accustomed splendor.

Let us imagine the magnificent procession which took three quarters of an hour to make its triumphal entrance! Behold the large number of Prelates, Bishops, Cardinals seated in the choir of the apse! Let us gaze for a moment at the resplendent throne of the Holy Father, at the brilliant costumes of the Prelates and the pontifical guards, at the thousands of electric lights which, replacing almost everywhere the traditional candles, shed their beams on all this splendor. Let us raise our eyes to the glory of light which, blazing above the pontifical throne, encircles the picture of the Most Holy Trinity, casting over it an incomparable glow; to those electric chandeliers radiating on the gilding of the pontifical ornaments, on the red damask, the armor, the arms and the uniforms of the guards, on the mosaics and marbles of the basilica, scintillations of superb effect! Add to all this the waves of harmony that poured forth from the vaulted choirs of the Sistine Chapel, the silver trumpets and the impressive *motives* of the Gregorian melodies—and who could hesitate to credit the enthusiastic accounts of this grand and never to be forgotten ceremony?

But we must finish our recital. Behold, then, the Sovereign Pontiff seated on his throne, the Sacred

College, the Patriarchs, Primates, Archbishops, Bishops and all the papal court around him. And now, the Cardinal Pro-Prefect of the Congregation of Rites presents himself, on his left the Consistorial Advocate, Commandant Octavo Pio Conti. The latter kneels before the Pope and, in the name of the Cardinal Pro-Prefect, supplicates His Holiness to deign to inscribe in the catalogue of the Saints the Blessed Gerard Majella and the Blessed Alessandro Sauli. In the name of His Holiness, Msgr. Vincenzo Sardi, Secretary of Briefs to Princes, responds that it is a very grave matter for which the Most Holy Trinity must first be invoked and the help of the Blessed Virgin Mary, of the holy Apostles Peter and Paul and of all the Saints must be implored. The Cardinal retires.

In the meantime, the Pope kneels, and the chanters intone the Litany of the Saints. The effect of this chanting was thrilling and grand. The crowd gathered in the basilica, alternating with the choir, chanted the invocations of the Litany. The witnesses declared that they felt as if the prayers of the Universal Church—at times agonizing, and then confident—were rising up to Heaven for help.

The chanting of the Litany over, the Holy Father, a lighted candle in his hand, re-seated himself on his throne. The Cardinal Pro-Prefect, with the same ceremony, renews through the Consistorial Advocate his petition, now making use of the formula *instantius*.

The Secretary of Briefs to Princes, in the name of the Pope, replies that the Holy Father, more than ever convinced of the gravity of the favor requested, wishes by other prayers to ask the light of the Holy Spirit. The Cardinal and the Consistorial Advocate retire. The mitre is removed from the Holy Father. He stands up before his throne, invites the Cardinals who surround him to fervent prayer, saying to them *Orate* ("Pray"), then intones the hymn to the Holy Spirit *Veni Creator* and kneels to the end of the first strophe. The hymn is taken up by the chanters of the papal chapel, and when finished, the *Oremus* is chanted by the Sovereign Pontiff.

The Pope again seated on his throne, the Consistorial Advocate renews his petition for the third time, this time "*instanter, instantius, instantissime*" ["insistently, more insistently, most insistently"]. At the last instance, the Secretary of Briefs to Princes responds that the Holy Father, now persuaded that the act is pleasing to God, wishes to proceed to the Canonization.

At these words, all rose, and Pius X, raising his voice in the midst of the impressive silence, pronounced the solemn formula which placed Gerard and Alessandro in the number of the Saints:

"Ad honorem Sanctae et individuae Trinitatis, ad exaltationem Fidei Catholicae et Christianae Religionis augmentum, auctoritate Domini Jesu Christi, Beatorum Apostolorum Petri et Pauli, ac nostra . . . . Beatos Confessores Gerardum Maiella et Alexandrum Sauli Sanctos esse decernimus, et definimus, ac Sanctorum catalogo adscribimus . . ."

"To the honor of the Most Holy and Undivided Trinity, for the exaltation of the Catholic Faith and for the spread of the Christian Religion, by the authority of Our Lord Jesus Christ, of the Blessed Apostles Peter and Paul and by Our own . . . We define and declare the Blessed Confessors Gerard Majella and Alexander Sauli to be Saints, and We enroll them in the catalogue of Saints . . ."

It was nearly ten o'clock a.m. when the infallible declaration of the Pontiff was uttered!

Further ceremonies followed, by which the Sovereign Pontiff decreed the expediting of the Apostolic letters to announce to the world the glory of the new Saints. He ordered also the festivities of the day to be registered in a public act.

These ceremonies over, the *Te Deum* was immediately intoned by the strong, sweet voice of Pope Pius X, and to it responded again the grateful multitude in a transport of enthusiasm.

The Cardinal Deacon afterward invoked the new Saints: *Orate pro nobis, Sancti Gerarde et Alexander, Alleluia!*—"Pray for us, Saints Gerard and Alexander, Alleluia!" Then the Pope chanted the *Oremus* proper. The Cardinal having recited the *Confiteor*, inserting after the names of the Apostles those of the two new Saints, the Sovereign Pontiff pronounced the formula of absolution and benediction, the name of the two heroes again upon his lips. To crown the ceremony, Cardinal Serafino Vanutelli published the Plenary Indulgence.

The Canonization was finished, and immediately after, the Pontifical Mass began with all the splendor of the usual rite. At the Offertory, the Postulator of the Cause, Reverend Father Benedetti, accompanied by another Redemptorist religious, went forward to present, the first a candle, the second a basket containing two doves. Then came His Eminence Cardinal Gotti with two Redemptorists, the one to present a candle, the other a basket with two turtle-doves; after whom His Eminence Cardinal Macchi with two other sons of St. Alphonsus came forward, one to offer a candle, and the other a basket in which were two little birds.

Would it be rash to assert that St. Gerard's Canonization, pronounced in the epoch in which we live, is in the designs of God a great lesson to the whole world? We think not. The Almighty, who had shown by brilliant prodigies that He desired a more solemn cult for His faithful servant, has thereby clearly manifested His divine intentions. Gerard, the magnanimous imitator of Christ Jesus, *magnanimus Christi imitator,* is to condemn by his sanctity and admirable life the vices of our age and to preach openly the virtues it seems to ignore.

Egoism under myriad forms, like a hideous canker, is corroding all classes of society. Men are seeking riches, honors, pleasures. They desire only these; they aspire only to them. The pursuit of these vain and miserable baubles consumes the energies of an incalculable number of souls.

The time seems past in which a man was contented with modest competence, was happy in his station. The rich man now wishes to accumulate more wealth; the man of moderate means wants to raise himself to the level of the rich; and the poor man, seduced by the rhetoric of the so-called friends of the people, feels his heart consumed by the fire of covetousness, hitherto unknown to him. The rich he hates; their wealth, their possessions he envies; and in his heated imagination he looks forward to the moment, the happy moment, that will establish for good and all, as he thinks, universal equality, and put an end to his misery and humiliation.

Once, men knew how to obey, how to submit to the yoke, how even to bear it with love, or at least without fretting and fuming. Not that there were no revolts. Since the revolt of Lucifer, since above all the revolt of Adam against the Creator, there has always been, and to the end of time there will always be such insubordination. But did pride ever attain the proportions which we behold in our day? Has there ever before been seen so pronounced a tendency toward absolute independence? "Neither God nor master" is the cry of a great part of society. They revolt against God and His law, against the Church and her ministers, against kings and their ordinances, in a word, against all authority.

And what shall we say of sensualism? It truly reigns as master, enslaving soul and body, enervating character, extinguishing the flame of noble courage. Of what do people dream in our day? Of feasts and pleasures. And what pleasures! O great

God! Of the pleasures to which the pagans gave themselves. Evil shamelessly displays itself everywhere, and the better to deceive the unsuspecting, every means is employed to hide its hideousness. There were not sufficient words to disseminate the accursed poison, so a new vocabulary had to be invented. Impurity is no longer the shameful sin, the sin that brought ruin to humanity and the destruction of Sodom. Oh, no! For our degraded race, it is only an amiable weakness! And to think that innocent souls have to live in the midst of this pestilence, constantly breathing an atmosphere reeking with sensualism!

Indeed, a great lesson was necessary for our age. It needed to see in all its purity, in all its brilliancy, the doctrine of the Divine Master put into practice in the life of one of those heroes whom the Church never ceases to show to the world and whom she will not cease to produce till the End of Time. The children of the Church themselves have need to behold the solemn condemnation of those vices that sully the lives of so many men and to be encouraged in the practice of virtue by brilliant examples.

The great lesson has just been given to the world; the example is now before the eyes of all mankind. Pius X, in elevating Gerard to the pinnacle of honor by Canonization, says clearly to the world that its salvation, its happiness can be found only in the imitation of Gerard's virtues, in contempt of perishable goods and in seeking the riches of eternity.

Gerard was poor in earthly goods. But far from

coveting the riches of the great ones of the world, he was ingenious in relieving the poverty of those poorer than himself. O ye rich, learn from Gerard to detach your hearts from your possessions and to give generously of your abundance to succor the innumerable forms of misery and distress that cover the face of the earth! And ye who are deprived of the goods of fortune, learn from him not to curse your condition, but to support it with resignation, nay, with joy and love!

Gerard knew but to obey! We have seen him submissive with the most profound humility and the greatest sweetness, to a cruel and heartless master who treated him harshly, abused him and inflicted on him real torture. We have seen him anticipating the least desires of those whom God had invested with authority over him. Let us read and re-read the examples of his admirable obedience, that in imitation of our Saint, we may learn to consider the authority of God Himself in all who command, that we may escape the spirit of independence which insinuates itself everywhere and which forms, little by little, that frightful and dangerous catalogue of revolts which aim at levelling all classes of society.

Lastly, Gerard was pure! His life was short, hardly thirty years! But his career was all holy. It shone from beginning to end with perfect innocence, with unstained purity. Mortal and fragile, in spite of the snares of Satan and the world he preserved stainless the immaculate robe of his Baptism; still more, as Leo XIII said in the Decree of Beatification, "A worthy emulator of St. Aloysius de Gonzaga and St. Stanislaus Kostka, Gerard appeared like an Angel of Heaven in the midst of men." We find in his life that he spared no pains to preserve his virginal purity; fasts, disciplines, mortifications of various kinds, all were employed for the preservation of the most delicate of all virtues. A great lesson for our age, enslaved by luxury and sensuality! May poor sinners sunk in the mire of impurity contemplate the pure, chaste life of St. Gerard! They will learn to despise and hate the shameful pleasures that so frightfully sully in man the very image of God, and which far from satisfying the soul in its quest for happiness, fill it with disgust, sadness and black despair.

You now see, dear Reader, that the life of our great thaumaturgus (wonder-worker) is most salutary for the unhappy times in which we live. Read it often and with the greatest attention. You will find in it strength and consolation. Make it known everywhere. Souls will learn from it that the accursed egoism which at present reigns everywhere must be trodden underfoot and that, according to their feeble ability and under the impulse of divine grace, they must imitate the holy life of Gerard. If you do this, believe me, you will perform a work of true zeal, you will contribute in your own sphere to the revival of purity of morals, to the renewal of the bonds of true fraternal charity, and you will help to put an end to the war between the classes; in a word, you will, according to the beautiful motto of our glorious and well-beloved Pope Pius X, labor to re-establish the reign of Jesus Christ on earth: *Omnia instaurare in Christo*—"To restore all things in Christ."

DEO GRATIAS ET MARIAE!

"THANKS BE TO GOD AND TO MARY!"

If you have enjoyed this book, consider making your next selection from among the following . . .

Prices subject to change.

Prices subject to change.

Story of a Soul. *St. Therese of Lisieux*................... 9.00
Catholic Children's Treasure Box Books 1-10............. 40.00
Prayers and Heavenly Promises. *Cruz*................... 5.00
Magnificent Prayers. *St. Bridget of Sweden*............. 2.00
The Happiness of Heaven. *Fr. J. Boudreau*.............. 10.00
The Holy Eucharist—Our All. *Fr. Lucas Etlin*........... 3.00
The Glories of Mary. *St. Alphonsus Liguori*............ 21.00
The Curé D'Ars. *Abbé Francis Trochu*.................. 24.00
Humility of Heart. *Fr. Cajetan da Bergamo*............. 9.00
Love, Peace and Joy. (St. Gertrude). *Prévot*........... 8.00
Père Lamy. *Biver*.................................. 15.00
Passion of Jesus & Its Hidden Meaning. *Groenings*........ 15.00
Mother of God & Her Glorious Feasts. *Fr. O'Laverty*....... 15.00
Song of Songs—A Mystical Exposition. *Fr. Arintero*....... 21.50
Love and Service of God, Infinite Love. *de la Touche*...... 15.00
Life & Work of Mother Louise Marg. *Fr. O'Connell*....... 15.00
Martyrs of the Coliseum. *O'Reilly*.................... 21.00
Rhine Flows into the Tiber. *Fr. Wiltgen*................ 16.50
What Catholics Believe. *Fr. Lawrence Lovasik*........... 6.00
Who Is Therese Neumann? *Fr. Charles Carty*............ 3.50
Summa of the Christian Life. 3 Vols. *Granada*........... 43.00
St. Francis of Paola. *Simi and Segreti*................. 9.00
The Rosary in Action. *John Johnson*.................. 12.00
St. Dominic. *Sr. Mary Jean Dorcy*.................... 13.50
Is It a Saint's Name? *Fr. William Dunne*............... 3.00
St. Martin de Porres. *Giuliana Cavallini*............... 15.00
Douay-Rheims New Testament. *Paperbound*............. 16.50
St. Catherine of Siena. *Alice Curtayne*................ 16.50
Blessed Virgin Mary. *Liguori*....................... 7.50
Chats With Converts. *Fr. M. D. Forrest*............... 13.50
The Stigmata and Modern Science. *Fr. Charles Carty*....... 2.50
St. Gertrude the Great............................. 2.50
Thirty Favorite Novenas............................ 1.50
Brief Life of Christ. *Fr. Rumble*.................... 3.50
Catechism of Mental Prayer. *Msgr. Simler*............. 3.00
On Freemasonry. *Pope Leo XIII*.................... 2.50
Thoughts of the Curé D'Ars. *St. John Vianney*........... 3.00
Incredible Creed of Jehovah Witnesses. *Fr. Rumble*....... 3.00
St. Pius V—His Life, Times, Miracles. *Anderson*.......... 7.00
St. Dominic's Family. *Sr. Mary Jean Dorcy*............. 27.50
St. Rose of Lima. *Sr. Alphonsus*.................... 16.50
Latin Grammar. *Scanlon & Scanlon*.................. 18.00
Second Latin. *Scanlon & Scanlon*................... 16.50
St. Joseph of Copertino. *Pastrovicchi*................ 8.00

Prices subject to change.

Holy Eucharist—Our All. *Fr. Lukas Etlin, O.S.B.* 3.00
Glories of Divine Grace. *Fr. Scheeben* 18.00
Saint Michael and the Angels. *Approved Sources* 9.00
Dolorous Passion of Our Lord. *Anne C. Emmerich* 18.00
Our Lady of Fatima's Peace Plan from Heaven. *Booklet* 1.00
Three Ways of the Spiritual Life. *Garrigou-Lagrange* 7.00
Mystical Evolution. 2 Vols. *Fr. Arintero, O.P.* 42.00
St. Catherine Labouré of the Mirac. Medal. *Fr. Dirvin* 16.50
Manual of Practical Devotion to St. Joseph. *Patrignani* 17.50
The Active Catholic. *Fr. Palau* 9.00
Ven. Jacinta Marto of Fatima. *Cirrincione* 3.00
Reign of Christ the King. *Davies* 2.00
St. Teresa of Avila. *William Thomas Walsh* 24.00
Isabella of Spain—The Last Crusader. *Wm. T. Walsh* 24.00
Characters of the Inquisition. *Wm. T. Walsh* 16.50
Blood-Drenched Altars—Cath. Comment. Hist. Mexico 21.50
Self-Abandonment to Divine Providence. *de Caussade* 22.50
Way of the Cross. *Liguorian* 1.50
Way of the Cross. *Franciscan* 1.50
Modern Saints—Their Lives & Faces, Bk. 1. *Ann Ball* 21.00
Modern Saints—Their Lives & Faces, Bk. 2. *Ann Ball* 23.00
Divine Favors Granted to St. Joseph. *Pere Binet* 7.50
St. Joseph Cafasso—Priest of the Gallows. *St. J. Bosco* 6.00
Catechism of the Council of Trent. *McHugh/Callan* 27.50
Why Squander Illness? *Frs. Rumble & Carty* 4.00
Fatima—The Great Sign. *Francis Johnston* 12.00
Heliotropium—Conformity of Human Will to Divine 15.00
Charity for the Suffering Souls. *Fr. John Nageleisen* 18.00
Devotion to the Sacred Heart of Jesus. *Verheylezoon* 16.50
Sermons on Prayer. *St. Francis de Sales* 7.00
Sermons on Our Lady. *St. Francis de Sales* 15.00
Sermons for Lent. *St. Francis de Sales* 15.00
Fundamentals of Catholic Dogma. *Ott* 27.50
Litany of the Blessed Virgin Mary. (100 cards) 5.00
Who Is Padre Pio? *Radio Replies Press* 3.00
Child's Bible History. *Knecht* 7.00
St. Anthony—The Wonder Worker of Padua. *Stoddard* 7.00
The Precious Blood. *Fr. Faber* 16.50
The Holy Shroud & Four Visions. *Fr. O'Connell* 3.50
Clean Love in Courtship. *Fr. Lawrence Lovasik* 4.50
The Secret of the Rosary. *St. Louis De Montfort* 5.00

At your Bookdealer or direct from the Publisher.
Call Toll Free 1-800-437-5876

Prices subject to change.